PRAISE FOR

CHOP THAT SH*T UP!

"If you read just one book this year of a soldier's true story, from enlisting as a private on the eve of Desert Storm to multiple combat deployments in Iraq and ascending to the pinnacle of the US Army's noncommissioned officer ranks in twenty-eight years of Army service, make it this book. US Army command sergeant major (retired) Daniel Pinion unflinchingly and with full transparency leads the reader through initial soldier lessons learned, leadership challenges and growth, monumental hardships, fear, courage, heartbreaking loss in combat, and family sacrifices.

"Ultimately, though, this extraordinary soldier-leader's story is about the unshakable and eternal bond of love that exists between soldiers, particularly those who have together risked everything and who bear the emotional, mental, and physical scars of war, as well those who have made the ultimate sacrifice. Anybody who can read this, particularly the dedicational prologue, and who does not shed a tear by the end simply does not have a pulse.

"Command Sergeant Major Pinion's story and that of his soldiers, peers, and leaders is beautifully and clearly written in a crisp, no-BS, no-sugarcoating, and straightforward style. At the same time, he refreshingly sprinkles his soldier's humility and sense of humor throughout the book. I strongly believe this book should be mandatory reading for all soldiers and soldier-leaders, aspiring or otherwise, regardless of rank. As for everyone else, I recommend it highly."

—COL Ralph R. "Rick" Steinke, USA (Ret.), former US Deputy Civil-Military Coordinator and Liaison to the Commanding General, ISAF Joint Warfighting Command, Afghanistan, Author of the Jake Fortina Series

"*Chop That Sh*t Up!* by CSM (Ret.) Dan Pinion meets the 3E criteria I have for must-read books! Easy to read, entertaining, and educational!! None of us are perfect, but after reading his draft I had to ask him: 'How the hell did you survive to become a command sergeant major?' Each chapter or story can be used to conduct a leader professional development session.

> —CSM Scott C. Schroeder, USA (Ret.), Former US Army Forces Command CSM, Author of *Behind the Colors: Where NCO Leadership Lives*

"Start to finish, *Chop That Sh*t Up!* is one of the most accurate tales of soldiering I've read yet, from unbelievable messed-up stuff while in garrison to endless zero-dark-thirty field training, red-tape bureaucracy, life lessons, and some real-life heroes in action. CSM (R) Pinion embodies the heart of a true warrior, exposing all the good, bad, and ugly of what it takes to be part of the strongest military force in the world. You will laugh and learn when the sh*t gets chopped up. You will also weep at the loss of comrades.

"Thank you, CSM (R) Pinion, for your life of selfless service and the embodiment of all the values and creeds of the US Army. We have never met, but thank you for taking care of the soldiers under your command! You were the father some of them may have never had. Thank you for treating America's sons as your own.

"God bless you, and God bless America!"

> —Nathan J. Gould, 101st Airborne Division (Air Assault), 3STB, 108th TNG CMD - Army Reserve, Charlotte Mecklenburg Police, Author of *Service to Civilian: A Journey through PTSD*, and Current Youth Pastor in Maiden, NC

"'Imperfect Perfection'—that is the definition of CSM (Ret.) Dan Pinion's incredible twenty-eight-year Army career. As a friend and a fellow 19D (scout), Dan was always my litmus test to judge my own career against in terms of assignments, leadership ability, job knowledge, and promotion timeline. He is the real deal who told it like it was (much to the chagrin of his leadership) and did not sugarcoat anything. Dan wore his heart on his sleeve, and his soldiers loved him for it. This book tells his story, while simultaneously telling theirs in a sort of self-deprecating humor that is infectious and entertaining. You will not be able to put this book down once you start reading it."

—CSM John A. Murray, USA (Ret.), Author of *Still Searching for Oz* and *Still Searching for Eden*

"*Chop That Sh*t Up!* is a true mastery of military realism that only this veteran can deliver! CSM (R) Pinion has created a military memoir with something unavailable anywhere else: corrective action. The entire career of this distinguished soldier is not only masterfully catalogued but also analyzed. *Chop That Sh*t Up!* showcases CSM (R) Pinion constantly learning from his mistakes and correcting himself by applying those experiences to better himself *and* his men. Valuable lessons are applied to combat proficiency, and he does it *naturally*. Learn by example and improve yourself [by] tracing the steps of a tried and tested combat leader. This is the absolute finest account of Army life available!"

—Aaron Michael Grant, USMC, Award-Winning Author of *Taking Baghdad: Victory in Iraq with the US Marines*

"A must-read for leaders and those who study leadership, as well as for those who have suffered the loss of comrades in arms. Humorous, honest, and heart wrenching along the way—these are truly life's lessons from a life well lived. Written by a true master of his craft in both hard and soft skills, who truly cares for those around him, this book should be on every military professional's bookshelf—dog-eared and highlighted.

—COL Mike Smith, USA (Ret.), Former Squadron Commander

"*Chop That Sh*t Up!* is filled with truth, emotion, and memorable 'free chicken' that would help any soldier—enlisted or officer—navigate a successful career all the way to retirement. I love how REAL the stories are. I read it and felt like I was hanging out with the CSM Pinion, having a beer and learning what the real keys to success are, instead of just slogging through all the field manuals and regulations. Thank you, CSM Pinion, for this timely and most helpful resource! I love this book!!! This is how a true cav. scout writes!"

—CH (MAJ) William Beaver, USA, Cavalry Squadron Chaplain, 3-1 Cav, Fort Benning, GA

"*Chop That Sh*t Up!* grabbed my soul and didn't let go! As we make our way through our careers in service to our country, we have all encountered different versions of CSM (Ret.) Dan Pinion's experiences. To see them put on paper and then to read the lessons learned that were tied to each of them through his deep reflection and genuine care was priceless and really brought it home for me. This is a MUST-READ for anyone in or out of uniform. It is a relatable treasure whether you are a civilian or in uniform and I thank you, Dan, for this gift."

—CSM Meara Brown, USA, 170th Military Police, Battalion Command Sergeant Major

"I've had the pleasure of observing CSM (R) Dan Pinion's leadership firsthand, and he has perfectly captured nearly three decades of experiences and leadership lessons in *Chop That Sh*t Up!* It is written just as he led: with enthusiasm, conviction, empathy, and discipline. CSM (R) Pinion's use of humor and reality are a perfect match that highlights the challenge of leadership. *Chop That Sh*t Up!* is a MUST-read for young leaders developing their own leadership style."

—COL Dan Enslen, US Army

"*Chop That Sh*t Up! Leadership and Life Lessons Learned While in the Military* is RAW, is ROUGH, and is deathly HONEST! CSM (R) Dan Pinion steps out of his armor and shares the highs and lows of an extremely successful military career. War isn't beautiful, but his love and lifelong dedication to his men and this country are. I am glad we met CSM (R) Dan and his family when we did; God doesn't make them like he used to."

—Mr. and Mrs. Robert and Holley Mackey, Founders and CEO of Heroes United Golf, www.heroesunitedgolf.org

"*Chop That Sh*t Up! Leadership and Life Lessons Learned While in the Military* is filled with comical humor of a seasoned combat leader. I witnessed the power of humor delivered by CSM (R) Dan Pinion in dire combat situations that provided a momentary stress relief for soldiers to accomplish the mission. Once the dust settled, I was able to understand the lessons of his stories—loyalty, duty, and love."

—LTC Mike Bajema, USA (Ret.), Troop Commander, F Troop, 1 CAV (BRT), 1 BDE, 1 AD, "Fantom 6"

"*Chop That Sh*t Up! Leadership and Life Lessons Learned While in the Military* and its exciting story shares an inside look at the life of a highly decorated, modern-day warrior dedicated to serving his country and his brothers-in-arms. The initial humor enticed me to keep reading and learning more about this extraordinary journey. We civilians need to read books like this to fully comprehend the sacrifices these heroes make for their fellow soldiers. They also deserve far more support when they get home. After enjoying it, we can put this book on a shelf, but for those who live through combat, there are NO shelves. Read CSM (R) Dan Pinion's story and you will understand!"

—Richard LaMotte, Author of *Follow His Lead*

"I truly loved *Chop That Sh*t Up! Leadership and Life Lessons Learned in the Military*. It was written in a way that made it so easy to follow CSM (R) Dan Pinion's journey through the military. Having been in the NJ National Guard from 1963 to 1971, in the 50th Armored Division Headquarters Company, 'Jersey Blues,' I understand the importance of following the rules. That sometimes leads to an inability to care about the men under your charge.

"What stood out to me was Daniel's ability to 'lead with compassion.' It is a very valuable talent that many in the military don't understand. It became apparent toward the end of the book that Daniel's compassion for his men took a very deep toll on his life. As a man who ran his company for forty-nine years, I learned RESPECT wasn't an automatic—it had to be earned; and Daniel earned that RESPECT from his men. I believe that those skills were directly responsible for his successes, but as I said earlier, I think they also led to Daniel's PTSD.

"*Chop That Sh*t Up!* humbly showcases Daniel's ability to be fair but firm, and how his men followed him. Yes, they followed him. He was always right there, leading. That is CSM (R) Daniel Pinion.

"Daniel, thank you for sharing your life with us and for giving us a glimpse into the life of a combat soldier. Also, thank you and every one of your men for their service."

—Mr. Gene Stull, President and CEO of Stull Technologies

"Any success I enjoyed as a young lieutenant and combat platoon leader was greatly due to the outstanding NCOs that I worked for during those fifteen months. The once Sergeant First Class Pinion belongs in those ranks. We were an unlikely pair, both prone to honesty in a war that was anything but and often at odds. We gelled as a team and together brought our soldiers home. It was my honor to again be paired with CSM (R) Dan Pinion. I was the executive officer (XO) and Dan the first sergeant as we helped an outstanding commander get those soldiers ready to go right back into the fire of war.

"*Chop That Sh*t Up!* and its collection of stories represents a life and career of an accomplished NCO who, in the words of the great Robert A. Heinlein, 'labored to make men out of boys.'"

—CPT Troy Gordon, USA (Ret.), Former Platoon Leader and Executive Officer, "Red 1" and "Fantom 5"

Chop That Sh*t Up!
Leadership and Life Lessons Learned
While in the Military

by CSM Daniel L. Pinion, USA, (RET)

Published by

köehlerbooks™

3705 Shore Drive
Virginia Beach, VA 23455
800-435-4811
www.koehlerbooks.com

CHOP THAT SH★T UP!

LEADERSHIP AND LIFE LESSONS LEARNED WHILE IN THE MILITARY

CSM DANIEL L. PINION, USA, (RET)

VIRGINIA BEACH
CAPE CHARLES

To my wife, family, and soldiers, who will always be first in my heart. To my friends, who "get" me and still love me. To the behavioral health professionals who saved me when I needed saving.

And to our heroes on overwatch in Fiddler's Green, I look forward to the day we are together again.

TABLE OF CONTENTS

FOREWORD

W hoever said "We are all the heroes of our life stories" has not read this book or met CSM (Retired) Dan Pinion. It is clear from the beginning to the end of *this* story that Dan's heroes are the soldiers he served alongside. So, I feel compelled to say that not only is CSM Pinion also one of the heroes of this story, he is the hero of many stories, to include my own.

When I knew him best, he was First Sergeant Pinion, the senior noncommissioned officer in our brigade reconnaissance troop (BRT), F Troop, 1st US Cavalry. Until the Sunni Arab tribes near Ramadi, Iraq, had their "awakening" and joined our side, the "Ready First" Brigade Combat Team (BCT) of the 1st Armored Division was up against a fanatical enemy in near total control of one of Iraq's largest cities. Because we lacked sufficient combat power to clear Ramadi and hold our gains, our forces were spread ever thinner as we systematically cleared areas of the enemy. So, "Fantom" Troop became my mobile reserve, which I sent wherever enemy activity was hottest or threatened our progress. This effectively kept it in the thick of the fighting throughout our fourteen-month combat deployment, most of it spent in what was then considered the most dangerous city in Iraq, the intended capital of the fledgling Islamic State in Iraq's "caliphate." I am convinced that without the skill, courage, and sacrifice of our Fantom troopers, our offensive would have ground to an early halt.

For such an important organization, the BRT was ridiculously small—less than sixty soldiers organized into two platoons mounted on HMMWVs. But they were by far the best-trained and best-led company-sized formation in the entire Ready First Combat Team of nearly 4,000 soldiers and punched way above their weight. Even after the ranks of the Ready First swelled to over 6,000 with the attachment of a reinforced Marine rifle battalion and additional Army battalions from other brigades and divisions, and despite the BRT suffering nearly 50 percent casualties, the most of any unit, it remained our best—a direct reflection of its leadership. If you read carefully between the self-effacing lines of this book, you can see how then 1SG Pinion's superb leadership qualities kept it an effective fighting force throughout the deployment. You can also see the personal toll this took on him.

Some may read this book as a collection of war stories, but it is really a love story. CSM Pinion's love for his soldiers is unmistakable as he fights the enemy, the elements, and the Army's infamous red tape on their behalf. In this series of vignettes, it is clear his love for his soldiers grew until it was put to the ultimate test in Ramadi, where he was forced to sacrifice the soldiers he loved for the sake of our brigade's mission. I know the pain of those terrible days haunts him still.

Although it is a very personal story, this book is also a useful source for anyone seeking to understand how the US Army as an institution persevered for years in a war that it was not winning. It was able to do so because small-unit leaders like Dan Pinion held platoons, companies, batteries, and troops together long enough for their officers to figure out how to defeat the enemy, and probably longer than we had a right to expect. Just as centurions were the backbone of the legendary Roman legions, our NCOs are the main reason America has the greatest Army in history, and they're better than anyone who hasn't seen them in combat can ever appreciate.

As Dan did, American NCOs lead our soldiers with knowledge, courage, compassion, and humor every day. But perhaps the most important NCO skill is their ability to teach, to pass along hard truths they've gained through experience. Although CSM Pinion is now retired, he continues to teach others. Once an NCO, always an

NCO. His moving story about a life dedicated to his soldiers in peace and war is full of hard truths we can all learn from. And no matter what he says or thinks, I can say with some authority, CSM (Retired) Dan Pinion is a hero.

Scouts Out! Ready First! Iron Soldiers!

LTG Sean MacFarland
US Army, Retired
Bulverde, Texas

PROLOGUE

"What are you going to do with your life? You can't play baseball forever."

I grew up average in almost every way possible. Although my mom divorced my biological father when I was little, I grew up in a two-parent household from age five and count my stepfather as my dad. I have a twin sister, two younger brothers, and cousins who lived only thirty minutes away from us growing up. It takes a village to raise a child, and we had that with our family and community.

I considered us middle class. Big house with a yard, woods for days behind us, a friendly and safe neighborhood, and hardworking parents who seemed to make everything possible for their kids. For example, every year we went to Florida on vacation to see our grandparents. It was expensive for six people to fly down on vacation for a week, but my parents always made it happen. On the way home from Florida each year, my dad, myself, and my middle brother, Matthew, volunteered to give up our seats because flights were always overbooked. This got us three free tickets, suitable for a year or another trip to Florida.

My mom couponed during the week with my aunt Barbie and then woke me up every Sunday to help deliver the Sunday paper while listening to Elvis on the radio. My dad, who to this day never sits still, worked in the garage or at work from 6 a.m. until 11 p.m. almost daily to help us make ends meet—I also think he simply liked tinkering with cars and listening to the 8-track player.

I was taught to hunt, fish, explore, dig fence posts, garden, build retaining walls, etc. The end of the school year meant going to the local flea market and picking out new work boots and a maul to split firewood. My dad would cut down the trees, my sister, Debbie, and I would load the wood and bring it back, and in the summer, I would split the firewood while my sister stacked it. On one side was last year's wood, dried out for the coming winter, and we would split and stack next year's wood on the other side.

My cousins and I loved sports, and our favorite was baseball. I felt I was destined to play for the New York Yankees one day. We would play catch, pitch simulated games, play baseball with a tennis ball, wiffleball, etc. Athletics were easy for almost everyone in our family. I was a leftie and had a great curveball in high school, but I was lazy, so although I was mentally tough and physically athletic, I lacked the discipline to make my dreams come true.

My relationship with academics was the same. It was easy, and I was generally intelligent, but I didn't understand why I needed to do homework when I already understood the subject. This landed me in summer school for my sophomore year of English despite my getting near-perfect grades on all tests. Riding your bicycle to and from school in the summer while your friends goof off changes your perspective on homework.

So, why the Army?

Well, although my grandfather, Frank Richards, served his country in World War II, and my uncle George served in the Army in Hawaii during the Vietnam War, there wasn't really a culture of profound pride in the Army or serving our country in the house growing up. We respected those who served their communities, but it wasn't openly communicated. We simply worked hard, had fun, and made ends meet.

However, as I neared the end of high school, my dad finally asked what I wanted to do with myself when I graduated. He and I were cutting wood on the property where *Friday the 13th* was originally filmed. It was a Boy Scout camp, and my dad's friend Ollie was the caretaker there when he wasn't working as a state trooper or in the National Guard.

Truthfully, I had no idea what I wanted to do. I had no mechanical ability like my dad, was lazy when allowed, and hadn't applied to colleges yet. Some colleges wrote me about baseball, but I hadn't signed with anyone yet. I needed something to jump at. I was having fun the way things were.

"Talk to Ollie when he gets here. He'll know someone in the Army," my dad said.

Within seven days of that conversation, I signed up with the New Jersey National Guard as a 19D cavalry scout, a reconnaissance specialist. I was a dream for the Army recruiter. I didn't do drugs, I aced all the exams, had no criminal history, and was very athletic. I signed up with no bonus and didn't ask for anything special like Airborne or Ranger School. I didn't put much thought behind the process or what I was about to sign up for; I leaped blindly into the future.

Basic training was terrific. It was sixteen weeks long because we were in one station unit training (OSUT), which combined basic and advanced training. I excelled in every task, loved the structure and discipline, and didn't get too wound up when drill sergeants yelled at me or our platoon. I was selected for a leadership position in week three of training and stayed in charge throughout the rest of the cycle.

Before I shipped off to basic, Uncle George had taught me how to shine boots, so my boots always looked incredible. I could outshoot anyone in the troop on the machine gun and other weapons and began learning to call cadence when we marched. This gave me a new level of self-confidence. I was tired every night, after many hours of training, but I woke up refreshed and ready to go every morning. I simply loved it. Even better was reporting to the pay officer at the end of each month, who gave us a paycheck. I couldn't believe they were paying me about $500 to $700 a month. I even wrote my mom that they were giving us too much money for this.

The build-up for Desert Storm was starting, making life good for us. We had three hot meals a day so they could send the packaged meals ready to eat (MREs) overseas to the soldiers. War on the horizon also gave us a sense of purpose in what we were doing and learning, and I drank up all the "Be all you that you can be" Kool-Aid the Army was selling.

I graduated in December and went back home to New Jersey. I left as a 6'1", 165-pound kid and came back an inch taller and almost 200 pounds, a lot of it muscle. My shoulders were broader, and I looked good. We did our usual family celebration and returned to our everyday lives. Except I couldn't, because I still didn't know what to do. The National Guard was one weekend a month and two weeks in the summer. What to do with the rest of my time?

I did what any cool high school graduate would do. I went to my local high school basketball game to show everyone how cool I was and see the ladies. As stupid as it sounds, this was where I realized I needed to be a soldier full-time.

Before every game, the national anthem is played. Everyone stands with their hands on their hearts. But soldiers turn toward the music or flag, and we stand at attention. Our bodies are rigid, betraying no movement or sound. The problem is that no one else follows those rules.

The day I visited my old high school, the student section and adults stood, and most placed their hands on the hearts, but they all kept talking and laughing. Some sang with the music, but most were disrespectful. The anger burned inside me. How could they act this way? That moment, at that game, changed my life. The next day, I found another recruiter and began the process of moving from the National Guard to active duty.

After a few weeks of paperwork, I reported to Fort Ord, California, on 14 Feb 1991 and haven't looked back. I served our country as a soldier for the next twenty-eight years and four months.

I deployed to countless countries, fought enemies in the name of America, and served alongside some amazing heroes.

This book is dedicated to those years of service. It combines crazy, stupid stuff I did and the lessons I learned. It also honors the heroes we lost in combat. This is their story too.

CHAPTER 1

CHOP THAT SHIT UP!

You learn very quickly about responsibilities when you join the Army. Some are clearly important, like signing for and maintaining weapons, night vision goggles, and military vehicles. Other times your responsibilities include cleaning latrines. As a young private first class at my first duty station, a latrine would shape the rest of my career.

From February 1991 to October 1992, I was a member of the 3rd Platoon "Wolfpack," Alpha Troop, 2nd Squadron, 9th Cavalry Regiment, 7th Infantry Division "Light Fighters" in Fort Ord, California. This prestigious platoon had the honor and duty of maintaining the second-floor barracks common area latrine, used by forty to fifty soldiers. Every morning, our first sergeant (1SG) would inspect the barracks to ensure we met the standards of cleanliness. If not, you could expect a cleaning "GI party" that night, supervised by our noncommissioned officers (NCOs), who would not be happy.

The first lesson I learned was the importance of ensuring your soldiers are prepared for the mission or inspections. I used to wonder out loud why the NCOs didn't come before the inspection to make certain we were ready. Instead, if by a slight chance we failed the inspection, the NCOs would destroy us. Have you ever tried to clean the shower floor by low crawling? Clean a toilet with your toothbrush? As one of the lowest-ranking guys in our platoon, I took it upon myself to begin inspecting the area prior to the first sergeant's arrival. I kicked soldiers out of the latrine and meticulously worked my way from the shower area to the sinks and down the toilets to the door.

This was how door guard became my additional duty. The platoon used to rag on me for taking charge and bossing people around, but I was tired of uniforms getting ruined and constantly buying new toothbrushes. My punishment from them was to stand at the door of the latrine and greet 1SG Stanley when he arrived. I didn't take this as a punishment, though. While everyone else turned and ran at the sight of a senior NCO, I used the opportunity to crack jokes and hone my speaking skills. I enjoyed offering up a "What a great day it is, First Sergeant" or a "Is that a new flattop haircut you have there? Looking sharp today, First Sergeant!" Yes, I was that guy, and I am not ashamed to admit it. I enjoyed it and saved money on toothbrushes simultaneously.

The joke was on them until one fateful morning. I had just finished making my bed corners and correctly spacing the hangers in my locker when my roommate, Cornelius, came in yelling for me.

"Pinion, get in here and fix this!"

Cornelius was an easygoing guy from Miami who taught me a lot about life and different cultures. For him to be yelling meant something big was up.

As we hustled to the latrine, 1SG Stanley was screaming at 2nd Platoon about how bad their stairwell was. At our latrine, I spotted my gunner and roommate standing over the first stall toilet, peering down into it. They opened a hole so I could get in between, and I saw the problem.

We were staring at the biggest turd I had ever seen in my life. Whoever deposited this monster needed to see a doctor to get their butthole fixed because it had to be torn up. I can't do this turd justice. It was so big that it was sitting on the bottom of the toilet bowl, and it could easily touch each side of the rim. It was longer than a M7 bayonet, if that helps.

"Pinion, this is yours to fix!" my gunner ordered me as we heard

1SG Stanley slowly progressing from the stairwell to the NCO latrine at the end of the hall. Only the hallway left, and then us. It would take minutes at least to fix this.

I jumped inside the stall and performed immediate action on the toilet. Immediate action is when you address a malfunction with your weapon system to make it work again. For a rifle, we learn SPORTS: slap the magazine upward, pull the charging handle to the rear, observe for ejection of the round, release the charging handle forward, tap the forward assist, and squeeze the trigger. In this case, it was much simpler. I reached down to flush the toilet.

The handle depressed, the water began to drain in its familiar swirling pattern, but the turd just sat there, refusing to budge. Water gushed all around it. It was like a water fountain statue. We heard 1SG Stanley beginning his journey toward us. I did the only thing I could think of: I shut the door and locked it. With hindsight, my subsequent actions would have been different, but I was nineteen years old and about to fail an inspection. This would cost us our free time, require extra laundry to clean up the Battle Dress Uniforms (BDUs), and of course I would have to replace another toothbrush.

All that low crawling in basic training paid off as I escaped under the stall and took up my position at the door. The other platoon members were positioned at their stations throughout the latrine. I checked my uniform, and everything was ready.

First Sergeant Stanley was a 6'3", broad-shouldered man with an airstrip-style flattop haircut. He was drafted into the Army during Vietnam and proudly displayed his draft letter on the wall behind his desk. A UH-1 Huey door gunner in Vietnam, he claimed he had been shot down three times during combat. He looked like he could kill you by looking at you.

Alcohol might have been his only flaw, and back then, it was tolerated. If he called for a platoon sergeant meeting after lunch, we would get released early because they were going fishing. If we made it until the end of the day, he would generally be holding on to the guidon bearer's shoulder or guidon staff during formation to avoid falling over. Despite this, he was among the best leaders I have ever observed in the field and training.

So here he came, head scanning left to right, checking the hallway floor, making sure 1st Platoon had waxed it correctly. The clear coat glistened. The wax between the tiles had been scraped clean by soldiers bending forks from the mess hall. First Sergeant Stanley was meticulous, ensuring no wax spots were on the baseboards. The first sergeant stopped at the fire extinguisher to ensure it was full and the expiration date was suitable.

A month before, we had decided to get drunk and expend the fire extinguishers on the floor. We placed a wall locker at the end of the hall, ensured our Kevlar helmets were on, and ran down the hallway at full speed, sliding headfirst into the locker, attempting to see who could put a hole in it first. None of us ratted out the others, so we all paid a steep price.

"Good morning, First Sergeant. Welcome to our fine dining establishment. So clean you can eat off the floor." My bullshit mode was in full gear this morning.

"Shut up, Pinion, and get out of my way! Everyone has failed so far, and I don't see you bucking the trend."

We were screwed.

"At ease!" I yelled, and everyone inside the latrine snapped to parade rest. This is to indicate respect when an NCO is the senior person entering a room.

"Carry on, troopers," he commanded under his breath.

First Sergeant Stanley immediately moved toward the first stall, as was his routine. "Why is the door shut? Who thinks it's okay to take a dump during my inspection? Pinch it off and get out of the stall, trooper!"

"First Sergeant, it's empty," I calmly stated over my right shoulder while still stationed at the door entrance. "It's broken."

"What's the matter with it?" 1SG Stanley asked, and here I made a mistake. I had yet to learn that the first sergeant was responsible for the maintenance and work orders for the buildings in our unit. This was about to get ugly.

"It won't flush, First Sergeant," I hesitantly responded.

I'm not sure if the seven Army core values had been published yet, but we fully understood the importance of integrity. Technically, I was maintaining that value. After he banged on the door, we realized the first sergeant was not going to give up.

"Open it up, Pinion!"

Oh no, here we go.

I crawled back under the stall wall and glanced at our enemy. He was still there, with a hint of a smile forming. *You son of a bitch!* If I saw any soldier walking like his butt hurt, I was going to kick it for this. I unlocked the door. As it swung open, I held the door against the stall wall with my back and stood at parade rest with 1SG Stanley on my left and the toilet on my right.

"Holy shit!!" the first sergeant screamed as a few soldiers behind him giggled.

"Roger that, First Sergeant," I said defeatedly.

First Sergeant Stanley squeezed into the stall next to me, me at parade rest and him staring at the most giant shit in the history of soldier turds. He reached over and hit the handle. Nothing. The big, smiling turd refused to move.

First Sergeant Stanley turned his cold eyes toward me. "You know what you have to do, Pinion?"

"No, First Sergeant."

First Sergeant Stanley held his right hand in front of my face and formed the famous knife hand used by every NCO and drill sergeant during their career—also used in a karate chop. It is when you take your hand and extend your fingers and thumb straight and touch each other (fingers and thumb extended and joined). Since it is viewed as disrespectful to point a finger and scream at someone, the way around it is to use the knife hand technique.

First Sergeant took his hand from my face, turned toward the toilet, and, still looking me dead in the eyes, chopped his hand *in the toilet*!

"You have to chop that shit up!" he said confidently.

The other soldiers in the latrine were gagging or full-out laughing now. I was in shock but still at parade rest, refusing to look at the hand-to-hand combat taking place in the toilet. First Sergeant Stanley stared at me the whole time.

He finally lifted his hand from the destruction, reached over, and hit the toilet handle. The most beautiful sound of swirling perfection took place, and the itsy-bitsy, chopped-into-a-thousand-pieces turd drained away. The first sergeant straightened up and stared into my eyes again.

"Pinion, this is a life lesson here today. During your career, you will hit many obstacles that won't go away on the first try. When that happens, you can give up and walk away or simply roll up your sleeve and CHOP THAT SHIT UP! Understand?"

"Yes, First Sergeant," I replied just as 1SG Stanley wiped his combat-proven hand on my left arm and shoulder.

After his hand was clean, 1SG Stanley winked, left the latrine, and said we had passed the inspection. Meanwhile, my entire platoon was busting up laughing at me, reenacting the hand wiping.

"I am going to change my top. I will meet you at formation," I stuttered.

At first, I was in shock, and was not looking forward to the endless jokes. But in the end, a fantastic thing happened: I learned a huge lesson that day. One of the reasons I made it to command sergeant major in the United States Army was that I never let any obstacle stop me from completing the mission. I simply rolled up my sleeve and CHOPPED THAT SHIT UP!!

CHAPTER 2

LETTER OF REPRIMAND

I n October 1992, I reported to Friedberg, Germany, where I was assigned to a reconnaissance scout platoon in 4th Battalion, 67th Armor Regiment. This was very different from my job at Fort Ord, where I was genuinely light and served as division reconnaissance for the 7th Infantry Division. Here I would learn to complement heavy units and tanks.

I arrived to a highly capable platoon. Each NCO was seasoned with years of experience, and most had served in Desert Storm. I was a young corporal (CPL) who needed to prove himself. In California, I'd had my own vehicle crew, but I had to wait my turn here, so I was assigned as the platoon sergeant's (PSG) gunner. Typically, you put the best gunner on the platoon leader's (PL) vehicle, but you put the vehicle commander in waiting on the platoon sergeant's vehicle.

We were going to gunnery immediately, so I would have my first taste of the field with them. Gunnery is where your unit shoots every weapon type they own while progressing toward qualification through multiple tables (levels). First you qualify on your individual weapon, then as a vehicle crew, and finally as a section and platoon.

In California, gunnery meant sleeping under the stars and driving to different ranges daily. We swam and washed in the creek running through the training areas. In Germany, things went a little different. We deployed to another post called Grafenwoehr, stayed on cots in the barracks, and drove to a range daily. The battalion would set up a "canteen" area in the dining facility at night, and you could drink two beers a night. I was going to like Germany's version of the "field."

Grafenwoehr was established in 1907 when a prince of Bavaria decided the area was best suited for the training of their army. It was also where Hitler and his Nazi army trained, and you can still walk up the same tower where he stood to watch his soldiers conduct military drills. Now the area is used by multiple countries to train and ready their forces.

However, I would not join my platoon right away. Because I was an NCO, I was assigned as one of the bailiffs for a soldier in pre-trial confinement for stabbing one of his roommates after a drunken argument. I and the other bailiff, SPC Mark Hopkins, stayed back to escort him to his court-martial.

Sort of funny, but we decided to go early to post, and all of us got fresh haircuts. We drove in military vehicles and wore our formal "Class A" uniforms. The soldier wasn't in handcuffs, so we were more like escorts. We all sat simultaneously to get haircuts, but the soldier being court-martialed finished ahead of us because he got his head shaved.

He paid, and we told him to wait outside the barber shop as we finished up. Lo and behold, we finished, and he was gone. Oh shit! After only one month in Germany, my buddy Mark and I had lost our soldier. We scoured the post exchange and attached stores but couldn't find him. Finally, we decided to sit down and think this through. Then we would call our sergeant and tell him what happened.

We sat at Burger King to formulate a plan. Suddenly, a few tables away, the accused soldier asked us, "What are you guys doing? Come sit with me." He was eating two Whoppers, and his tray was loaded with food. He had no intention of leaving, but if he was being sent to prison, he wanted Burger King.

Good for him, I thought.

The court-martial went as expected, and the soldier was reduced to private, E-1, and sent to confinement in Mannheim, the only

Department of Defense level 1 correctional facility in Europe. We escorted him to the correctional facility and transferred him to the guards, then proceeded to meet our platoon at gunnery.

Once at Grafenwoehr, we started our training progression, which involves a lot more than just showing up, jumping in as a crew, and executing your crew qualification table. One of the progression tables was to shoot the M2 heavy machine gun, .50 cal, at paper targets and then undertake field familiarization fire. It taught us how to zero and use traverse and elevation (T&E) devices while becoming proficient at firing the weapon.

Unfortunately, our battle buddies, the tankers, also had .50 cal weapons, and they outnumbered us. We were told to run the range for them too, which meant three days' worth of ranges. We were going to fall behind on our tasks. But orders are orders, so we planned to run three straight range days for them, and on the fourth day, we would shoot.

Running a range involves a myriad of tasks. Being the new guy, I got the job of greeting people as they entered. I would show them where to park and then read off the tasks, conditions, standards, ammunition count, personnel on the range, etc. After my briefing, I escorted them to where they needed to go.

After three days, everything was running smoothly. The tankers were shooting well, and we helped mentor them through their deficiencies. This allowed me time to learn my weapon as we prepared to shoot on the fourth day. Finally on the fourth day, our turn arrived, and I was standing near the ammunition point at the tower's base on range 312. Mark, the ammunition NCO, grabbed me and said all hell was about to break loose.

We heard the platoon sergeant and platoon leader arguing something fierce up in the tower. Apparently, another batch of tankers were coming to the range to shoot, and we had to support them. SFC Matthew Gram, the platoon sergeant, was pissed and letting the platoon leader know it. The platoon leader didn't back down, though. He was a big boy and stood his ground.

They descended the stairs and headed for the wood line—for some wall-to-wall counseling, we assumed. No one tried to stop them, and we all gathered around to figure out who would win. We couldn't see or hear anything, and after a few minutes, they came back, walking side by side. They simply wanted a personal conversation without us, and everything seemed calm now. Finally, SFC Gram stopped at the ammo shack and told me to prepare for some tankers coming out to shoot.

I ensured my numbers were correct, updated the ammo count, and prepared for their arrival. I inspected the gate guards and confirmed the TA-1 military field telephone and wire were run correctly and working so I could call the tower when they arrived. Within an hour, the two-and-a-half-ton trucks pulled up with another company of tankers in the back.

I gave my speech, showed them where to park, verified their numbers, updated my book, and called the tower. Then SFC Gram came out to brief everyone on the conduct of the range.

SFC Gram started, "Gentlemen, welcome to range 312, where today we will assist you in completing tables one through four for the fifty-cal machine gun. Before we start, if I could have everyone who conducted PMI stand to my left, your right, and everyone who hasn't on the other side. This will assist us in setting up our training stations to help you." Game time; I knew exactly what was about to happen.

Before you go to the range in the Army, you must be familiar with the weapon and certified to shoot. We do this through pre-marksmanship instruction (PMI). Unfortunately, hardly any unit does this correctly and cites "lack of time" or other priorities as an excuse. PMI is typically half-assed training given by an unqualified teacher who barely covers the basics. But you need it to go to the range.

Of course, not one single tank crew had conducted the pre-training as required. I understand they were focused on making sure their tanks ran correctly and prepping to shoot main gun rounds from their barrels, but this was embarrassing. It was nice that they maintained their integrity, though, as many soldiers lie about PMI when they show up to a range.

"Get the hell on your trucks and off my range! Return to your company and tell the commander and first sergeant to do their jobs so I can do mine," barked SFC Gram.

SFC Gram turned around, smiled, and left. It was now up to me to assist the tankers off the range. They asked if he was serious. "Dead serious," I said, and off they went.

I returned to the ammo point as SFC Gram explained to the platoon leader that he couldn't allow them on our range without proper training first and it was his duty to enforce standards and discipline. Granted, the first three days, we never asked anybody the PMI question and just mentored the crews through the tables. However, a point was being made; apparently, their stroll in the woods didn't resolve everything.

So, we started to shoot and progressed through the tables relatively quickly until I heard someone yell for the reporting NCO. The gate guard had someone at the gate who needed me, so I briskly walked over (you cannot run on a range).

It was our battalion commander (BC) and command sergeant major (CSM). I had little experience with senior leaders, but seeing them together and unannounced meant we were in for a world of hurt soon.

"Good afternoon, sir and Sergeant Major, and welcome to—"

"Shut up, Corporal, and get the platoon sergeant NOW!" snapped the command sergeant major.

"Roger that, Sergeant Major and sir. Please park at the VIP sign while I get him."

The gate guard had already picked up the TA-1 and called the tower for me as I handled ground guide duties for the battalion commander's HMMWV. SFC Gram came around the corner as they exited their vehicles.

"SFC Gram, did you tell a company of soldiers to leave the range and report back to their commander and first sergeant and for them to do their jobs?!" questioned the battalion commander.

"Yes sir, but I didn't say it that nicely," said our ballsy platoon sergeant.

"Get your platoon leader and yourself to my office in thirty minutes, understood?" the battalion commander ordered.

"Yes sir, but we're running a range," SFC Gram replied.

"Not anymore you aren't," the commander yelled, and with that, they jumped in the vehicle and left.

"Get our vehicle ready, Pinion. I'll get the platoon leader."

We drove back to the battalion HQ without saying a word. We parked, and SFC Gram and the platoon leader went inside. The driver and I tried to guess what was happening but had no idea. About thirty minutes later, they came out, got in the HMMWV, and told us to drive back to the range. Again, nothing was said.

Later that night, while we were staying at the range 305 barracks and getting ready to play Risk, SFC Gram asked me if I knew what had happened today.

"No, Sergeant. People did not follow instructions, and you told them to get lost," I guessed. By the way, SFC Gram was a senior NCO, sergeant first class, E-7. When addressing an NCO, you call them "Sergeant," but when talking about them, you use their full rank—in this case, sergeant first class.

"Yes and no, Pinion. I was wrong. Our job as leaders is to train soldiers, and I didn't do that. We should have trained them and then talked to their leadership after. It is what we do."

"I understand, Sergeant. Did you get in trouble?"

"Not really, brother. I received a local letter of reprimand again. It's like the seventh in my career. It's higher than the counseling statement we give you guys. They're simply telling me they're serious about the incident. All good NCOs get one, and you will too!"

And that was that. Our platoon sergeant would get another

reprimand a few months later, which is the next story, but he was still viewed as the best NCO in our battalion. Our platoon won "Best Scout Platoon" every year, was the only platoon to have a 100 percent pass rate on a new soldier development test the Army designed, and he developed and mentored some of the best soldiers I have ever served with.

I never got a reprimand in my career, but I should have earned a whole bunch. I was fortunate my leadership gave me some great ass-chewings instead.

The lesson learned was to take advantage of every opportunity to train soldiers, no matter what unit they are with. Make them as good as you because you might depend on them one day when it counts. This still gets me in trouble today, but as a civilian working for the Army, when I see something being done wrong, I still tactfully try to correct and teach. A whole infantry platoon at Fort Benning knows what I'm talking about.

CHAPTER 3

TAP, TAP, TAP OF THE RAZOR

This is a quick story, but I still smile every time I think about it. SFC Matthew Gram was tough but fair, and I modeled a lot of my leadership style on what I learned from him. However, as shown in the last story, he occasionally rocked the boat and got in trouble. This is about another one of those times.

The phone rang at about 0200 hours in the morning.

"Second Lieutenant Pinion, this is Sergeant First Class Gram calling from the Military Police station. Can you hear me, *Second Lieutenant* Pinion?" my platoon sergeant asked, sounding nervous.

"Yes, I can hear you, Sergeant. Did you say you're at the MP station?" I asked, trying to wake up.

"Roger that, Second Lieutenant Pinion."

He again emphasized the title. However, at the time, I was still a corporal, E-4, and not in charge of anyone. My platoon sergeant was an E-7—way higher than me.

The enlisted grades go from E-1 to E-9. A second lieutenant is technically above all enlisted ranks, though. Even the lowest officer rank and grade, O-1, is higher than the command sergeant major, E-9. This is because officers receive their college degrees, attend officer training, and swear an oath to lead us. I chose to be enlisted, so this structure was fine with me. Plus, a second lieutenant would never try to tell a command sergeant major what to do. I guarantee that would end badly for the young lieutenant.

But my platoon sergeant was clearly trying to tell me something, and despite the early hour, I understood the assignment. I was now an officer in the United States Army, senior to my platoon sergeant, and I needed to get him out of trouble at the MP station.

"I am on my way, Sergeant. Second Lieutenant Pinion is on the way," I emphasized to let him know I understood and agreed to the mission in case anyone was listening.

Now I had to figure out how to impersonate an officer. I was young enough to look the part, and I was in shape, so I just needed to dress like one. For some dumb reason, penny loafers were in style; I had a pair, and every officer wore them, so I got lucky. I threw on some jeans and a collared polo shirt—Pinion to the rescue.

Just like in the civilian world, impersonating someone of authority is illegal. I knew what I was doing was wrong and did it anyway. I arrived at the MP station and walked in, shaking my head. As soon as I saw the desk sergeant behind the glass window, I demanded, "What the fuck did my sergeant do now? I just arrive to a unit, and the next thing I know, I'm dealing with issues from my battle buddy. I did not expect my *platoon leader* time to be spent babysitting a senior NCO."

"I don't know, sir, but you must sign for him, and he will be released to your care. Thank you for coming in so quick," said the desk sergeant.

I don't know why he didn't verify me in the system, and quite frankly, I didn't care. It sounded like they wanted him gone, and I was here to help. I scribbled an incoherent signature on some paperwork and met SFC Gram as they brought him out. He was clearly embarrassed and ashamed of the position he had put me in; however, he was released, so all was well.

We got in the car, and it was silent for a few minutes. I thought he was going to apologize, but he started with a question: "Do you tap your razor in the sink when you shave?" he asked.

Now, I was barely twenty-one years old and barely shaved as it was, but when I was growing up, everyone who shaved tapped their razor to remove hair on it.

"Roger that, Sergeant."

"I fucking *hate* that," he screamed. "I am trying to sleep when I wake from the guy living above me." SFC Gram began to motion with his hands. "All I hear is *tap, tap, tap . . . tap, tap, tap.* So, I went upstairs and rang the doorbell, and when he answered, I said, 'Please stop fucking tapping your razor on the sink. I can't sleep because of you.' You know what he did, Pinion?"

Rhetorical question, because I was about to answer when he continued, "He told me to get lost and began to shut the door, so I grabbed him and choked him. Turns out, Pinion, he's an MP and called his buddies, and now I am arrested for assault, but this fucking clown should be arrested for shaving like an idiot." He was dead serious.

I didn't know what to say, so I simply asked, "What are you going to do now, Sergeant?"

"I'm screwed because the report will be on the command sergeant major's desk in a few hours, so I need to talk to him."

We pulled up to our housing area, and I let him out. As he was about to shut the door, he leaned back in and said, "I put you in a tough spot; plus, I don't like our current platoon leader, so thanks. I'll get this sorted out. See you at PT."

As I was about to back out of the parking spot and head to my street, he motioned me to roll down my window, which I did.

"Pinion, I can see you as an officer." He turned and walked away.

To this day, I'm not sure what he meant.

My platoon sergeant never got in serious trouble, and I thank the early '90s for that. You could never get away with that stuff today. Again, he was the best platoon sergeant I ever had, bar none. He had his faults, but he genuinely cared about us and spent every day making us better. He was the main reason we were the best scout platoon in Europe, and he is why I survived combat many years later. He taught me how to be a soldier, and of course, I made mental notes of his very few flaws so I could try to be better than him. I turned out okay, so thank you from the bottom of my heart, SFC Gram.

CHAPTER 4

THE NIGHT I MADE SERGEANT, E-5

I was very fortunate to always have leaders who pushed me to improve. As a result, I was laterally appointed to corporal rank by June 1992, after only sixteen months of service. I don't know if I was legally allowed to be promoted that fast, but I have paperwork that says I was a corporal and an NCO in the United States Army. I was put in charge of my first soldiers and given a truck to command. I was nowhere near ready and still didn't know my head from my fourth point of contact, but my leaders believed in me, and I worked hard to prove them right.

In Germany, my scout platoon was terrific, and they continued pushing me to improve and progress. However, I was never genuinely mentored on how to get promoted above the E-4 grade. Becoming a sergeant required you to go to a promotion board and work to obtain points. If the Army needed 100 new sergeants, they would lower the promotion point level in my specialty until the highest 100 people on the Order of Merit list made it.

One day, my platoon sergeant looked at me, dumbfounded, and asked, "Why the heck aren't you a sergeant yet, Pinion?"

"I have no idea, Sergeant," I replied.

He then sat me down, went through my promotion point worksheet, and painstakingly showed me every area where I was failing. I was a great scout but needed to improve professionally and personally—for instance, take college credits and correspondence courses, improve my physical fitness score, etc. He immediately made me sign up for college classes and courses to catch up to my peers. It paid off. I made the cutoff score and would be promoted on 01 December 1994. Becoming a true NCO and a sergeant, E-5, is a huge transition and accomplishment for a young soldier.

That year was a good one, and we would end it with a bang. In July, I had married my German wife, and we spent three weeks of our honeymoon traveling to see family in New Jersey and Florida. Our scout platoon was the best in Germany for the second straight year, and I had reenlisted to spend six more years in the Army (with a picture of Elvis as the backdrop; he had been stationed in Friedberg). The Army gave my wife and I a rent-free place to live (housing area), and my leaders lived down the street; life was good.

Then Staff Sergeant (SSG) Roger Harmon asked me for a favor. I'm not using his real name to protect him from embarrassment. SSG Harmon was small in stature, slim, good at his job, quiet, and mostly kept to himself. He and his wife separated, and he moved into the barracks about two weeks before my promotion ceremony. His wife was also a staff sergeant; she worked in the Personnel Services Division on the post and had reviewed my packet for promotion. Roger suspected she was cheating on him, and his suspicions turned out to be true.

Our scout platoon would go to the field for three weeks of training, then come back for one week to clean equipment, catch up on medical appointments, and let people know we were still alive; then we would go back to the field. We did this for four straight months. After that, we would go to the field for two months: one month of gunnery and one for our validation exercise. Our validation exercise would be against opposing forces (OPFOR) and show that we were ready for combat. As if that weren't enough time away, our platoon was always picked to stay after the validation exercise to augment the OPFOR for their next rotation. Add all that up, and we were never home. This naturally led to marriage issues.

Anyway, SSG Harmon lived two streets below mine, and as we were closing out formation one day, he asked, "Corporal Pinion, do you think when you go home from now on, you can swing down my street and see if any strange cars are parked in my spot? I know my wife is cheating on me, but I need better proof. Can you call me in the barracks if you see anything?"

"No problem, Sergeant," I responded. This didn't seem too hard of a task, and I felt bad for him, so I drove up his street for the next two weeks. I never saw any strange cars.

On 01 December 1994, a Thursday, I was officially promoted to sergeant by our battalion commander, LTC Martin E. Dempsey. It was a massive deal for me personally and professionally, and it was about damn time—and time to celebrate. I rushed home to be with my wife, hoping to get lucky as part of my celebration, but it had become a battle drill to swing by SSG Harmon's street, and instincts took me the same route that night. This time, I saw a car in his spot that was not his wife's. I jotted down the description and made my way home.

My wife and I had a great meal, and after dinner, I called the barracks and let SSG Harmon know what I saw. He thanked me and congratulated me again on my promotion. Phone call done, dinner done, uniforms laid out for tomorrow, and boots shined, it was time to celebrate with the wife. We fell asleep, everything was perfect . . . and then I heard a knock on the door.

It was nearly 0200 hours, and I had to be up at 0500 to get ready for PT. Nevertheless, I got up, put on my PT shorts and brown T-shirt, and answered the door. There was SSG Harmon with a big-ass camcorder (remember, this was 1994), asking for help.

"Pinion, I need a witness, please. The car is still there. You found it; I would like to videotape it there and have you witness it."

"Roger, Sergeant. Let me get my shoes on." Mistake number one or two. I should have stayed out of the whole thing from the beginning, but here we were.

I kissed my wife, telling her I would be back soon and that I was helping a friend. We then walked the two streets to his house, and SSG Harmon videotaped the car parked in his spot.

"Look, Pinion, there's a light on in my house. Let's go to the next apartment building and see if we can see into mine."

Mistake number three.

The houses were apartment houses—or stairwell houses, as we called them. SSG Harmon's apartment was on the third floor. All the houses on the street were on a slope, and the stairwells had big windows to let in natural sunlight. The stairwell doors were supposed to be locked, but no one wanted to fumble for keys when carrying groceries, so people left them permanently unlocked.

We entered the house, walked up four floors, and sat down. SSG Harmon's dining room had curtains, and they happened to be pulled open. Light seemed to be coming from a lamp in a room nearby. But there was nothing to see, no movement. We sat there for almost an hour. It was nearly 0330, and I needed to shave and get a few minutes of sleep, so I told SSG Harmon I had to go; he had what he came for.

We left the house and headed back up the sidewalk toward my house. Roger was a few feet in front of me, filming the car again. We passed the entrance to his apartment building, and for some reason, I stopped and looked back over my left shoulder. Mistake number four.

In that precise spot, I could see through the living room curtains and make out two people on a couch, and it looked like they were having a lot of fun. I took a step forward and looked: nothing. Took two steps back: nothing. I had stopped in the exact spot necessary to see his wife and another man having sex on the couch. I couldn't make this crap up.

"Sergeant, come here," I whispered, positioning him where I had stood. He was shorter than me, but eventually, I guided him on target.

"We got her!" Roger exclaimed, apparently happy about catching his spouse cheating and having sex on their couch. "Pinion, I can't get a good video of this. We have to get closer." He moved closer to the house.

How the hell are we going to do that? I thought.

"We have to climb up to the balcony. Our curtains don't fall to the floor, and I can film underneath."

"I'm not coming. I saw what I needed to see! I am going home," I said in frustration.

"No, you are not, Sergeant!"

As soon as someone stops using your name in the Army and only says your rank, you are royally fucked. I would learn in a few hours how immoral, unethical, and illegal this order was, but at 0400 in the morning, I was not thinking straight. Mistake number five.

We began our climb to the third-floor balcony. We got to the first balcony with no issue. I reached up, grabbed the floor of the second-floor balcony ledge, and pulled myself up. Reached down, grabbed SSG Harmon's camera, moved so he could pull himself up, and repeated for the third floor.

I got to the third-floor balcony first and had no idea how we did this so quietly. There were flowerpots and crap on the balcony floor, yet somehow, we dodged them.

I lay flat on the floor and saw SSG Harmon's wife going to town on another man's body part. To make it worse, Roger was now lying on my back with his head next to my ear and some big-ass video camera next to me. He hit the record button and started collecting his evidence. I closed my eyes and wished for this nightmare to be over, but no such luck.

"Oh yeah, look at her, Pinion. She does that so well," Roger whispered into my ear. I grew physically sick as this lady's husband narrated the porn scene unfolding before us.

"Sergeant, get off of me! I'm going to be sick." I pushed him off and got up, knocking into some of the flowerpots. This obviously startled the people inside.

I began climbing down, not concerned with SSG Harmon or the

people inside. I jumped from the second floor to the ground, which was muddy from the December weather. As I got up with mud all over my legs, SSG Harmon yelled for me to catch the video camera. I readied myself, and just as SSG Harmon dropped the camera, the first-floor balcony door opened.

"What the hell are you doing, and who are you?!" screamed a soldier.

I jerked my gaze toward the soldier, who was obviously pissed, and the camera hit the ground. I picked it up, hoping it was not busted. Roger jumped down, did a tuck and roll, and popped up.

"We got her, George!" he happily said.

"What the fuck, Roger! Get out of here," the neighbor demanded.

We started to leave and heard "I'm calling the MPs!" from SSG Harmon's spouse above. Roger raced back toward the stairwell. I thought he would attack her, so I followed him.

SSG Harmon got to the third floor first and knocked on the door opposite from his apartment. I was huffing and puffing, trying to catch up, when our first sergeant answered. Well shit, now I knew where the first sergeant lived, and he didn't look happy to see me.

"We got her, First Sergeant." Roger rushed inside the first sergeant's house.

The first sergeant said, "What the fuck, Pinion, get in here!"

It was almost 0430, and people were slowly getting up for the workday or praying for another hour of sleep. Meanwhile, we were in the first sergeant's living room, and SSG Harmon was trying to get the video camera to work while explaining what we had done.

The first sergeant gave me a look I will never forget. I felt my career was over right there. We heard people leaving Roger's apartment and figured it was the guy his wife was fooling around with. The first sergeant waited a few minutes for the guy to leave, told SSG Harmon to shut the heck up, and ordered me to go home.

"I suggest, Corporal Pinion, that you think about this and what you want to do after the Army," said the first sergeant.

"It's Sergeant Pinion," I corrected him. Mistake number six. He'd called me corporal and asked me to think about my next career because this one was clearly done.

I ran home, showered, shaved, and got ready for work. I told my wife everything was fine and then drove to work, extremely scared and running a thousand different scenarios through my head.

Our platoon sergeant saw me, asked how the celebration dinner went, and then asked if there was anything I wanted to share.

"Not really, Sergeant, but I think I messed up."

"No shit, Sherlock. You and I will see the command sergeant major in fifteen minutes, so fill me in right now!" he ordered.

I told my platoon sergeant the story and saw the disappointment on his face. He didn't yell, though, which was a lesson well learned for the future. Genuine disappointment is far worse than yelling. The yelling came from the command sergeant major. He ripped me a new asshole and then some. I was on his color guard team and one of his favorites, but that morning I was the biggest piece of garbage to ever set foot in the Army. I felt horrible.

They told me to go home and that they would let me know my fate soon. Thankfully my wife was at work when I got home because I broke down crying like a baby. How the hell did I end up in this position? Why did I let a superior talk me into doing something illegal and immoral?

That night, my squad leader came over and filled me in while laughing and yelling at me. My platoon sergeant had smoothed everything over and promised I would be on every shit detail from then until eternity. SSG Roger Harmon was immediately removed from the platoon.

Roger's spouse got in trouble, lost rank, but stayed in the Army. Her lover, a buddy from softball, was demoted and chaptered out of the Army. He was also married.

I never got in trouble and can thank every one of my leaders for protecting me. I learned to never follow immoral, unethical, or illegal orders again, no matter who gave them to me. From there on out, I questioned authority if I needed to. I also learned that people mess up. Which screwups teach lessons, and which ones should be punished? Disappointment is way worse than anger, especially when you genuinely care for your soldiers and they know that.

I will never forget the night I was promoted to sergeant, E-5.

CHAPTER 5

MIKEY AND THE WHORE

"Fist" was his nickname because he had a head the size of your fist and multiple chins that looked like knuckles. "Mikey" was his most commonly used name—also made up.

Mikey was from West Virginia and was raised by a deeply religious father who hated that Mikey's sister was a lesbian. I remember Mikey telling me that he hit rock bottom when his dad made him sleep in the barn and he woke up to rats eating his face.

As to why he was sleeping in the barn, well, Mikey didn't like school much. One day, he didn't want to take a test, so he called in a bomb threat. But the principal recognized his voice. That maneuver landed Mikey in juvenile detention for a little bit and a few nights in the barn when he got out. Mikey decided that day in the barn that he needed to improve, so he finished school and joined the Army as a 19D cavalry scout. Mikey's first assignment was Friedberg, Germany, in our scout platoon, where he was assigned as my driver.

Most soldiers in the barracks spent the nights studying, shining boots, drinking, or all of the above. On weekends they would drink and march down to the local club, the Studio—or as we called it, the "Booty Hole"—to try to meet women and get lucky. Most soldiers struck out with the ladies, and Mikey was no exception.

When that didn't work, the soldiers would take a train to Frankfurt and visit the red-light district. Prostitution was and is still legal in Germany, and the Army didn't crack down on that behavior as much as we should have. Each Friday, I asked the soldiers what they were doing on the weekend and went through risk mitigation to ensure they weren't being completely stupid or unsafe. I quickly learned that payday weekends meant Frankfurt, and other weekends meant the local bar and disco club. I would also quiz the soldiers on their knowledge of scout tasks at the end of the week and assign homework like my first NCO, SSG Timothy Butler, had done to me. Mikey could name every country western night in every European club but could not tell you the six fundamentals of reconnaissance (there are seven now, but in my time, there were only six).

But one Friday, I quizzed the squad, and Mikey did amazingly. Vehicle ID, fundamentals of reconnaissance, spot report format, etc. He nailed them, and I was so proud.

"Great job, brother. I am proud of you for putting effort and time into this. Take Monday PT off. I will get it approved!" I declared.

"Thanks, Sergeant. I owe it to my girlfriend. She's been helping me study, and when I do good, I get laid!" Mikey proclaimed.

"Did you have to pay?" asked one of the soldiers, and a few more crude comments followed.

"Knock it off, guys. I'm sure she is nice. You should bring her to the platoon party next weekend, Mikey."

"Thanks, Sergeant, I will," an overjoyed Mikey replied.

Some of the others tried to say something, but I thought they were going to make fun of Mikey for having a girlfriend, so I gave the almighty command "AT EASE," which basically means "Shut the hell up; I'm in charge" when used in this context.

They all scurried away, laughing their asses off. I would find out why soon enough.

The following week, we were doing lane training and supporting a tank company as they ran through maneuver drills. We conducted a quick route reconnaissance for them and then provided overwatch as they practiced across open fields.

We ran through this lane five or six times in one day. On the last iteration, I thought it would be good to see how Mikey handled the vehicle as the commander. This was what my leaders did for me, and I learned a lot from it. Mikey had to read the map and talk on the radio. Very easy, and I thought Mikey knew the route. So we switched places, and I started driving with Mikey reading the map.

Halfway through the exercise, I asked Mikey which way he wanted me to turn at an intersection coming up in one kilometer (just over half a mile). We reached a choke point, and I was about to ask again. On the left was straight uphill, on the right was a cliff, and ahead was a tunnel. I looked over to ask Mikey which way—and he was having a seizure, clutching the inside of the doorframe with his hands, his body rigid.

I yelled at the gunner, SPC Goad, to signal the vehicle behind us since I couldn't reach the radio hand mikes on Mikey's side. I drove as fast as possible through the tunnel and located a safe place to pull over on the other side.

We stopped; I jumped out and ran around the back of the vehicle to get to Mikey's side, yelling and waving for the rear vehicle to help. My section sergeant, SSG Tracey Heap, came running up as I pulled Mikey from the HMMWV. Mikey was still convulsing, and we had no idea what to do.

We yanked off his flak jacket (body armor). Unfortunately, we yanked it over his head, which dislocated one of his shoulders.

"Don't let him swallow his tongue," ordered SSG Heap.

I made a rookie mistake and put my thumb in his mouth. Like most of us, Mikey chewed tobacco, and it was all over my hand. And when I placed my thumb over his tongue, Mikey clamped down and bit my thumb down to the bone. I screamed.

Thankfully, some passing Germans saw us, stopped ahead at the next town, and called an ambulance. The ambulance arrived as Mikey was recovering from the seizure. I spoke German, so I jumped in the ambulance with Mikey and headed to the hospital.

The doctors did their thing. I had my thumb stitched while Mikey was attended to in another room. About an hour later, Mikey came out with one arm in a sling and stated that he had been released.

"Doctors say I am okay now, but I need to see the Army doctors as soon as possible. They don't know how I dislocated my shoulder. They popped it back in place but said it needs to be checked out also, Sergeant."

We signed all the paperwork and walked back to base (less than one kilometer), met the platoon, and got Mikey settled in his room. We assigned a battle buddy to watch him and got some chow hall food for him.

"Don't worry, Sergeant. I'll call my girlfriend. She'll take care of me!"

"No problem, Mikey, but tomorrow, I'll take you to sick call to see the doctor."

"Roger, and thanks again for saving me today," a very grateful Mikey responded.

The next day, Mikey was told he couldn't drive a vehicle for six months, carry a weapon, or do anything military related until time had passed and no issues arose. Now I was short a driver.

Friday came, and I asked the soldiers what their plans were.

One soldier said, "Mikey, tell him."

"Sergeant, my girlfriend said she can come to the party, but we might be late because she is working and coming from Frankfurt."

"Great. Thanks, Mikey. I look forward to meeting her."

Our scout platoon was very tight. Our wives got along, and most of us lived in the same housing area; it was a good bunch of people. We held the BBQ on one of the open picnic area spots we often used for PT. Music was playing, there was food, drinking, football, etc. Everyone was laughing and having a good time when suddenly things got quiet—except for my soldiers, who started laughing.

Mikey walked up with his girlfriend. I don't want to get told off for describing a stereotype; suffice to say, I thought she looked like a prostitute.

I grabbed my gunner. "Where did Mikey find this girl? She looks like a whore!"

"From the red-light district, Sergeant," my gunner said, straight-faced and without hesitation.

"Fuck!" I had just realized why my guys kept laughing about Mikey's girlfriend.

Mikey introduced her to everyone he could. The wives looked like "WTF is happening," and the single soldiers were laughing. Then came my platoon sergeant.

"Pinion, get Mikey and his whore out of here right now! He said you told him it was okay to bring her."

"I did, Sergeant. I just didn't know who his girlfriend actually was."

"Learn your soldiers, Sergeant." And that was that.

I pulled Mikey to the side and told him she was not allowed there and that I was sorry. Mikey tried to make an excuse that she was not working, so it was okay, but obviously, I couldn't budge. With that, Mikey and his girlfriend left, and the party continued, but it wasn't much fun after that.

I drove some soldiers back to the barracks after the BBQ and went to check on Mikey. A satanic symbol has been smeared on his door in peanut butter and jelly, and next to it was a shirt impaled with scissors.

We opened the door and rushed inside to find Mikey lying against a wall locker in pain, crying. The locker was dented like he had been thrown against it.

"Sergeant, please take me to the hospital again. I think I hurt my shoulder again and maybe cracked a rib."

"Mikey, what the hell happened?" I asked.

"My girlfriend and I got in a fight, Sergeant, and she karate kicked me into the wall locker and then stole one of my shirts and slammed the door. Then she began chanting in another language and left after beating on the door." It was a good thing Mikey's roommate had been with me, or who knows how long he would have laid there, suffering.

Mikey was right: broken rib, and a messed-up shoulder again.

I realized I needed to learn my soldiers better, not yell, "At ease" when they were trying to tell me something, and I needed to understand Army values better for myself and my soldiers. I had made the prostitute feel bad by putting her in the wrong position, and I was the reason she kicked Mikey's ass. The worst part was that Mikey had lost his study partner.

CHAPTER 6

SHAKY JAKE AND THE HAND GRENADE

In fall 1995, the former Yugoslavian country of Bosnia-Herzegovina was out of control, with three Bosnian groups fighting each other. The Dayton Peace Accord was drafted and implemented to stop the war and ensure peace. Our unit would be deployed with the mission to enforce the accord and allow the people of Bosnia-Herzegovina to put their war-torn country back together again.

I continued to excel at my job, and after only a few months as sergeant, I was sent to the promotion board for staff sergeant. I had been quick to corporal, slow to sergeant, and, hopefully, extremely fast to promotable status for staff sergeant. When my section sergeant, SSG Heap, told me I was going to the board, I said, "I'll probably get promoted soon after the board, Sergeant. I keep track of my points, and I'll be in the top percentile for 19Ds."

"I recommended you for the board because I know you're ready to be a staff sergeant now," SSG Heap said.

This made me feel good coming from a leader I deeply respected. The next month, while at gunnery, I was recommended for promotion, and my crew reshot "distinguished" to put the icing on the cake.

In January 1996, we received word that our airborne forces had seized and secured Tuzla airport in Bosnia the month prior, and we would soon follow behind them. Our mission was to travel north and secure the south side of the Sava river for follow-on forces to arrive. The rest of the battalion would arrive a month later after traveling by rail and bus to Hungary. We would go to Hungary, pick them up, and escort them into Bosnia-Herzegovina.

Except our timeline was about to get accelerated.

On a Monday, our platoon leader came into the office and stated the battalion commander was required to be in Bosnia by the weekend. The commander needed an escort team, and our section was selected to go. The platoon immediately began helping us get ready.

While preparing maps and equipment, we discovered we had new types of radios (SINCGARS, or single channel ground and airborne radio system) for the mission, and I was given a forty-eight-hour class on how they worked. Then I taught the platoon. On Thursday, as we were preparing our trucks and equipment, we found out the battalion commander now wanted the entire platoon to go, so we had to expedite the other three sections to get ready.

By Saturday, we were in the motor pool, receiving the new radios and crew tents and prepping the vehicles to fly on a military aircraft. I think it was a C-5 or C-17. We drove to Rhein-Main Air Base, near Frankfurt, that afternoon with a scheduled flight out that evening.

Honestly, I don't even remember saying goodbye to my wife. I only remember packing everything according to the packing list with her helping me inventory my gear. Saturday was a blur; however, when we arrived at Rhein-Main, our flight was pushed until Sunday evening, so we left the trucks and equipment and took a bus back to our base.

The following day we were bused back to Rhein-Main, where we processed the necessary paperwork, loaded the vehicles on the planes, and waited to fly. We were nervous, but this was supposed to be a peacekeeping mission, and the only threat discussed was the thousands of mines in the country. Our maps were littered with red dots, with one red dot representing one to a thousand mines in that area.

We flew Sunday night, and executing the landing was pretty cool. The aircrew had us mount the vehicles so we were all in position when we landed. We landed, the ramp lowered, crews unleashed the tie-downs, and we drove off. Within a few minutes, the plane was empty and turning around to take off again.

The division commander, Major General William Nash, was waiting for us, welcomed our battalion commander, and briefly talked to us. He told us to get north, secure the south side of the Sava river, near a crossing site they were preparing, and then recon possible base camps for our battalion. We received ammunition, grenades, and sandbags for our vehicle floorboards, and off we went.

Now, in our scout platoon, we had ten HMMWV vehicles—typically with three soldiers per crew, but we were never manned 100 percent, so we had to get some soldiers from another unit to fill us out. Within the platoon, you had four sections, plus the HQ section. Two vehicles in each section, but you could cross-level crews to suit the mission.

The "lead scout" is the senior staff sergeant in the platoon, and he led us everywhere. This person is generally the most knowledgeable, but not in our platoon. SSG Heap was the most knowledgeable; and although junior in the rank of sergeant, I was, quite frankly, a better scout than the other squad leaders. Together, my staff sergeant and I were a dynamic duo with great soldiers underneath us.

Our lead scout was smart but quirky and absolutely could not handle stress; this was how he became known as "Shaky Jake." Jake's wingman was a sergeant who had recently been promoted to staff sergeant, but since we were over our allocation for staff sergeants but under for sergeants, he stayed as a wingman. People have different perspectives on who leads within a section. Some put the wingman in front (our platoon did this) with the staff sergeant vehicle behind to help command and control.

As we were about to leave for the mission, the lead scout informed the platoon leader that his wingman had left his maps in Germany. We were all scrambling to dig out extra maps to cobble together another set for him when the platoon sergeant told our section to lead us north. Then I was told that I was leading as the wingman. Fun times. I immediately got nervous, but I could read a map and knew my job. Everything ran smoothly, and we reached our objective without issue.

This was, of course, old-school navigation without GPS or blue force trackers. You had a map, an odometer, and a protractor. It helped that only one road went south to north in Bosnia, and all we had to do was follow it and not hit a minefield. Nearly thirty years later, while traveling for work as a civilian, I navigated the same road and can confirm that they haven't fixed anything. It still makes Pennsylvania roads and turnpikes look smooth.

We eventually completed our mission to secure the south side, found and established a base camp, Camp Colt, escorted our battalion teammates down to Bosnia, and helped find and mark too many minefields to be comfortable with. It was draining. No showers, either; we would heat a .50 cal ammo can full of water on our potbelly stoves and clean ourselves with a washcloth. It was cold, with about two to three feet of snow on the ground, which made mine detecting especially fun. Basically, it sucked. The stress was building, and tempers grew short.

Once the battalion was established at Camp Colt, they started implementing standard procedures for maintenance. We had grown accustomed to doing our own thing for the last month and a half, but now we would need to inspect our vehicles and request them to be dispatched for missions every seven days. This was a horrible idea because we could be out on a mission for seven to ten days without warning.

Shaky Jake didn't like it; it frustrated the crap out of him.

During one down day (no scheduled missions), we started our dispatch procedures. The vehicles and maintenance tents were located on the flight line, and I had just finished a mission brief for the following day and was heading to join my team.

As I approached the maintenance tent, two or three soldiers

jumped through the flaps. I heard screaming from inside and, being the idiot I am, ran into the tent—just in time. Shaky Jake was screaming at the maintenance sergeant: a master sergeant, E-8, and someone very senior to Jake. Shaky Jake had his back turned to me.

"I will fucking do it!" yelled Jake

"Fucking pull the pin," the maintenance sergeant yelled back.

What the hell is going on? As I came around Jake, I saw him holding an M67 fragmentation grenade. One hand was cupping the grenade and spoon, and a finger from his other hand was wrapped around the pull pin. The maintenance sergeant had both hands around Jake's.

I did what any dumb person would do and put my hands on top of theirs. So now the grenade was covered by six hands, and I yelled, "Everybody fucking calm down."

I had either startled them or found a commanding voice I didn't know I had, but they immediately stopped screaming and looked at me—three of us face-to-face and holding a grenade.

"Master Sergeant, please release your hands. Staff Sergeant, please let go of the pull pin gently. Give me the grenade, and both of you step back," I ordered.

They listened, and I secured the grenade. As soon as I had the grenade, I left the tent, yelling some nonsense instruction to the soldiers gathering to see what the commotion was. I range walked (speed walked) to our platoon tents, where I found the platoon sergeant and platoon leader.

"Shaky Jake lost his mind and pulled a grenade on the maintenance guy," I stammered.

"Where's the grenade?" the platoon leader demanded as he jumped up from his cot.

"Right here in my hand, sir."

The platoon sergeant also rose, took the grenade from me, inspected it (which I had failed to do), and set it down for safekeeping. Then they ran out, got Shaky Jake, and took him to his tent.

Jake was gone within one to two hours, and my section pulled his slack. He was sent to Mental Health for a few days, which is called Behavioral Health now since it rolls better off the tongue. No investigation, no sworn statements, nothing. A few days later, Shaky Jake returned, and all was forgotten. He never returned to the maintenance tent, though. We all pretended it had never happened, but I learned what stress can do to an individual. This would greatly help me years later in Iraq and Afghanistan.

When we returned from deployment nine months later, our platoon sergeant went to his next duty station, and Jake was named the platoon sergeant.

Impossible, we all thought. How long would Shaky Jake last?

Jake made it exactly one month before he went to the first sergeant's office and asked to be removed from the responsibility. I don't know what was said, but it must have been convincing because, within one week, they moved another NCO over from a different post.

Stress is hard, and it is essential to always know your soldiers, personally and professionally. We knew Jake stressed easily, but we only tried to help him after a significant incident during deployment. I also learned during that deployment that when the situation became stressful, it was up to me to calm things down. I learned to call people by their first names when shit hit the fan. It put them at ease and helped them focus on talking to me.

In later positions, I used these lessons to show my soldiers it was okay to have problems and acknowledge them. I was the first to make routine appointments with Behavioral Health, and I made sure my soldiers knew and saw—and more importantly, joined me. I also ensured that we never again did seven-day dispatches in the field or deployment; thirty-day dispatches always!

CHAPTER 7

DRILL SERGEANTS X AND Y

The Army provides a lifetime of great experiences and frequently uses lessons learned and vignettes to help you understand and benefit from someone else's mistakes. Sometimes the stories provide a good laugh, while others are very serious. This is not a serious one.

In 2001, I was a senior drill sergeant at Fort Knox, Kentucky, for 19D cavalry scouts. This excellent assignment prepared me for future challenges as a platoon sergeant and first sergeant. My two years of being a drill sergeant were coming to an end, and I had one more sixteen-week cycle before I was done. We taught basic training for nine weeks and advanced training for seven weeks, all together in one cycle. I served as both the senior drill sergeant and a platoon drill sergeant since we were shorthanded. But we were due to receive SSG Jason Bishop soon, as he was graduating from drill sergeant school. He had previously shadowed us for one cycle as we helped prepare him for school.

"Chubby" Bishop was a homegrown Kentucky kid from Covington. His nickname was "chubby Bishop" because we had two Bishop's in the Squadron. One was fit and athletic and one was a shit-talker and very cocky, and I was not sure if he viewed his drill sergeant assignment as an award or a punishment. I gave him the one piece of advice I have given every soldier planning to become a drill sergeant.

"Don't change who you are when you wear the drill sergeant hat. Whatever got you selected is exactly what the privates need to see. You are at the top of your MOS [military occupation specialty].

Don't change. You will fail if you try to become God with the hat on."

Bishop seemed to take the advice, and we got to know each other before he reported to the school. Drill sergeant school mirrored regular basic training at the time. It was nine weeks long, and you did everything a private would do. As a bonus, you had to memorize and recite pages' worth of drill instructions (modules). If you ever see or talk to a past or present drill sergeant, just ask them to pitch the "position of attention," then sit back and enjoy the next few minutes.

Our cycle began without significant issues. But as with any cycle of privates, there were some fascinating characters. Basic training is the ultimate melting pot of cultures, ideas, values, and beliefs. The privates soon learned we would break them down and build them back up as one team. Generally, after the first week, we saw who wanted to be there and who didn't.

Private (PVT) Schmitt absolutely didn't want to be in the Army. His mind was made up. I cannot remember where Schmitt was from, but he was a small, lanky kid, about 5'7" and 125 pounds soaking wet. He would routinely leave the barracks and hide from us—in the storage closets, taking long walks around the post, or in the boiler room for almost two days. We played hide-and-seek with Schmitt for about two weeks.

Chubby Bishop had been in school when we started, so he had no idea about Schmitt yet. We were getting ready for the first significant test for the privates, which we called gate testing. They would test all morning and afternoon on roughly thirty-five to fifty different soldier tasks. Once they passed, they would move to the next training phase. As we did every morning, we conducted our morning physical fitness, shit, showered, shaved, and moved to the mess hall for a wholesome breakfast.

Accountability is key with anything. Every time we had a formation, I would walk down the formation, pointing my knife hand and counting how many soldiers I had. Because of soldiers recycling to other troops, injuries, and privates who were chaptered out of the

Army, it was essential to keep our numbers straight.

The numbers matched before marching to chow. When we came out of the mess hall, I saw we were one short. I counted again, and now the privates had little smirks on their faces. Putting everyone in the front-leaning rest position (starting push-up position) fixed that as I did my third count.

"Who is missing, Privates? Bookworm, is our number still forty-seven?" I asked.

Bookworm was a private designated to help with the admin stuff. He kept the numbers up, adjusted duty rosters, etc.

"Drill Sergeant, you know who is missing. Private Schmitt went into chow but is nowhere to be found now," answered Bookworm.

Crap. Here we go again. I did a quick search inside and saw nothing; hide-and-seek had begun again. We continued our mission and marched to the test site. I reported Schmitt missing to my chain of command, and the drill sergeant at the barracks searched the usual hiding spots.

We tested all day and came back to the barracks around 1700 hours. No Schmitt. Our platoon had the highest passing rate in the troop, so we earned our first streamer to proudly display on our guidon staff. It was a big deal and allowed us to talk smack to the other platoons. I checked in with the duty drill sergeant, and still no Schmitt.

It was nearing the end of September in Kentucky, meaning it could either be eighty degrees or snow that night.

We marched to evening chow and afterward settled back into the barracks. We sent the privates to bed early that night to reward their performance, letting them shower and prepare at 2000 (8 p.m.) rather than keeping them busy until 2200 (10 p.m.). I was in my office writing performance counselings on each private in the platoon. We assessed them constantly and provided verbal and written feedback to let them see how they were progressing throughout their training. It sucked to do, but it was an essential learning experience. I took this with me even as a one-star general-officer-level sergeant major providing counseling to my soldiers.

I was almost done for the night when I heard the familiar three knocks on the door.

"Drill Sergeant, Private Jones requests permission to speak."

I had absolutely no idea who this private was. I spent the first few weeks learning my privates' names, hometowns, strengths, and weaknesses. This soldier was not part of our platoon or troop.

"Who are you, Private?"

"Drill Sergeant, I am from D Troop. We have KP [Kitchen Patrol] today, and we are all wondering if Private Schmitt is coming back."

"What do you mean coming back? What are you talking about? Get in here!"

Private Jones came in and explained that Schmitt had eaten his breakfast, turned in his tray to be cleaned, and then proceeded to help the KP privates by working at the pots and pans station.

"Schmitt cleaned all day until after lunch. We wonder if he is coming back because we left the pots for him after dinner, Drill Sergeant."

"Get out of here, Private. Schmitt is not coming back to help you guys anymore."

Well, at least we knew Schmitt was accounted for from 0700 until approximately 1400 hours today. I called the first sergeant and let him know the status, and we decided to do another search of the barracks. After an hour of searching, we called it off. Schmitt never made it more than a day or two gone, so we would surely see him tomorrow.

The next day came. Nothing. Another day. Nothing. Another week: nothing. Schmitt had successfully made it three weeks. In a way, I was proud of him. If he could make it to day thirty-one, he would be considered a deserter and dropped from rolls. He had about six days to go.

Meanwhile, Chubby Bishop had graduated from drill sergeant school and returned to us. He was off and running, and I began to back off platoon duties and focused more on the senior drill sergeant duties, some of which included scheduling transportation (when we didn't walk) and deconflicting chow schedules with other troops.

One day I was up at squadron HQ to speak with our senior operations sergeant about the chow schedule. He was talking on the phone, then paused and looked at me.

"Don't you own Schmitt?" he asked.

"No, Sergeant. He went AWOL a few weeks ago." I checked my watch and the date. "He is a deserter in three days."

"So sorry, brother. They found him. He's in Alaska. I'm talking to the Military Police station in Fort Wainwright, Alaska. He's standing in front of them."

I grabbed the phone and quickly got caught up. I described Schmitt to the officer on the other line, who confirmed it was him. Schmitt made it onto the post and went to the MP station, telling a great story of how he graduated the mighty B Troop, 5-15 Cav, basic training, and was on graduation leave in Alaska. He had been with his church group but got separated when he chased a bear away to keep the group safe, losing his wallet and ID cards in the process. He requested help getting his plane ticket, cash, and military ID again to report to his first duty station in Korea.

Because his story wasn't adding up, the officer at the desk found our number to confirm his identity. What timing for me.

"Arrest him, sir. He's AWOL from us," I clarified.

"Will do."

I then informed our troop HQ and told the first sergeant and commander what was happening. PVT Schmitt would be shipped back to us, and we would help process him out of the Army. The good news was our squadron commander finally agreed to process his chapter packet.

We received his flight information and knew he was flying in the day after next. Meanwhile, our privates would be shooting the MK-19 40mm grenade launcher machine gun and needed some of us out there since we were light cavalry experts and knew the systems the best. We decided the new guy should go pick up Schmitt. We were joking around with the other drill sergeants in the troop when I told DS Bishop to get ready to pick up Schmitt from the airport. All of a sudden, the chaos started.

"Do we really want to send Bishop? He is kind of small compared to Schmitt," one drill sergeant said.

"Schmitt doesn't like white guys, let alone drill sergeants," another said.

Bishop seemed to be getting mad, thinking we were serious.

"I'll do it. I stopped Schmitt last time when he went after the commander," DS Reyna said. Mind you, Reyna was about four inches shorter than Bishop and easily thirty pounds lighter.

"What the hell?! I got this!" Bishop yelled and stormed off. We were all laughing now, which made him angrier.

The day of Schmitt's grand arrival came, and we were at the MK-19 range when Bishop came up. He briefed the first sergeant on his tasks and ensured that everything was good to go. I was busy with the privates and didn't hear everything, but DS Rivera came up laughing.

"Battle, Bishop said he doesn't need backup. He's ready for Schmitt," DS Rivera chuckled.

We laughed and continued training. The next part was described to me by several sources: airport security, the MPs, and the drill sergeant on duty.

Bishop arrived at the airport with time to spare. His uniform and drill sergeant campaign hat looked sharp—and he had handcuffs and a police baton he'd borrowed from his local cop buddy. This wasn't going to end well!

Back then, we could go to the gates to meet passengers as they deplaned. Passengers arrived, and DS Bishop was trying to figure out who Schmitt was. He kept looking for big guys. Suddenly, this small, lanky kid came out with a top hat and a cane. Where the heck did he get that? Well, on the Alaska side, they did their job and got him on the plane. However, the plane stopped in Chicago, where Schmitt decided to go shopping. We had no idea where he got the money because all he had was a new ID card on him.

Schmitt pimp-walked up to DS Bishop and tapped him on the shoulder.

"Drill Sergeant, are you looking for me? It's me, Schmitt. Are you my chauffeur for the evening?"

DS Bishop lost it when he realized we were messing with him, and then his short temper exploded when Schmitt put his hands on him and asked if he was his taxi driver. DS Bishop grabbed Schmitt, threw him on the floor, and jumped on top of him.

Cuffing him on the spot, DS Bishop dragged Schmitt around with one hand on his collar and the other on the baton, which he held between the private's legs, essentially lifting him by the groin. Schmitt was on his tippy toes.

Airport security showed up, a crowd was forming, and DS Bishop said he heard two or three people say, "We love you, Schmitt. Stay strong; my dad is a lawyer. They can't force you back into the Army after serving four years for them." Or some crap like that. Who knew what story Schmitt was telling his fellow passengers?

DS Bishop smoothed everything with airport security and drove Schmitt back to Fort Knox. When they arrived at the barracks, he put Schmitt in the old arms room next to the duty desk. DS Reyna was on duty that night, along with two privates.

The enclosed arms room was about eight feet wide and ten feet deep. It was supposed to store our weapons during the cycle, but since all the barracks didn't have the latest security alarms, we couldn't use it. Despite not having an adequate alarm system, it did have bars like a jail cell. You opened the solid doors, entered the storage room, and closed the bars, which had a little window. You could issue weapons through the window while ensuring that no one could enter and steal something. In this situation, Schmitt was the weapon. DS Bishop placed a cot in the corner for Schmitt to sleep on.

However, DS Bishop couldn't let it go and continued talking

with Schmitt, just the two of them, while DS Reyna conducted his barracks checks.

Ring, ring. My home phone was loud as hell. It was midnight, and I had been on the verge of sleep. I had to wake up at 0400 hours to be in by 0500 for "lights on."

DS Reyna was freaking out. "Battle, get your ass in here now. This is messed up! The ambulance is on the way. Chubby Bishop knocked Schmitt out. He's unconscious."

"On the way. Call the first sergeant. Call the MPs. Don't say a word to anyone until I get there."

I threw on my drill sergeant sweats and sped to work. I lived only ten minutes away. The first sergeant was at least twenty out, so I had time to figure this out.

I got to the barracks as the ambulance was taking off. MPs were there. I ran inside and saw Bishop in handcuffs. Blood was on the floor, and DS Bishop was yelling that his hand hurt. He had a freaking tooth lodged in one of knuckles.

"Whose tooth is that?! Never mind. Don't say anything!" I shouted.

The MP had already read him his rights, which DS Bishop smartly invoked. (I don't care what anyone says. You have a right *not* to say anything. Why in the world would you waive that? That would save me years later as a sergeant major.) They decided to take Bishop to the hospital and left with him.

"Reyna, what happened?" I asked.

"Private, come here and tell DS Pinion what happened. Battle, I was doing checks and came down to this."

I will summarize the information I gathered.

DS Bishop was sitting with Schmitt in the "arms room" and said, "Schmitt, do you *really* want to get out of the Army? If so, there's an easy way to do this. You just have to hit me!"

The comment took Schmitt aback, but Bishop walked him through it.

"Hit me, and the Army will have you home in one week, tops."

After gathering some courage, Schmitt stood and took a half-hearted swing at DS Bishop, which didn't come close to landing. At this point, Schmitt was standing on one side of the room and DS Bishop on the other as a private from the staff duty desk watched in terror.

DS Bishop finally convinced Schmitt to take a real swing at him. Schmitt did so, with all his might. Bishop stepped back, watched the fist fly by his face, lunged forward in retaliation, and caught Schmitt square in the mouth with a tremendous punch that lodged the tooth in Bishop's knuckle. Schmitt was now knocked out and lying on the floor, the staff duty private was screaming for DS Reyna, and my phone was about to ring. Now you're caught up.

The first sergeant showed up, and we filled him in. He told me to check on Schmitt and Bishop and ensure both were okay. I arrived at the hospital and checked on Schmitt first. He was missing his tooth but smiling and happy, despite the swollen mouth. I asked if he was okay.

"Yes, Drill Sergeant. I get to go home now. I assaulted a drill sergeant, and he defended himself, but it was all my fault, and I accept full responsibility for my actions. Please let me know when I can go home."

At my limited maturity stage, I wasn't going to argue with his version of events. Sounded good to me. I then checked on Bishop, whose hand was really swollen. He was okay—scarred but okay. Of course, we were all scarred at that point.

PVT Schmitt was released and processed out of the Army shortly after that. DS Bishop stayed in the hospital for two weeks because his hand became infected. The rest of us got off extremely lucky, which I am a little ashamed of to this day, and it provided a huge lesson learned for me going forward. Overall, the incident went away quietly.

About a month later, one of our drill sergeant candidates returned from graduating.

He kept calling me DS Y, and Bishop was DS X. Finally, I was like, "What the heck, battle?! What's up with the name?" He hysterically shared how famous we were in drill sergeant school now; when they had classes on lessons learned and what not to do, our story was the main vignette. Thankfully, they didn't have all the details as explained here, but they had enough.

What did I learn from this? For starters, I failed at the Army values. Duty: do what's right, legally and morally. I should have given everyone all the facts and never put my battle buddy DS Bishop in that situation in the first place. Personal courage: I allowed Schmitt to share his recollection of events and accepted it, knowing it was wrong. I should have made him tell the truth. Nothing good comes from hiding it, and I grew determined to never again be afraid to say what needed to be said or hide facts or details from my soldiers, units, and leaders I dealt with or briefed.

These candid and sometimes hurtful truths would rub many a leader and subordinate the wrong way going forward. Leaders in the Army beat around the bush too much and try to play nice. Before senior-level briefings, I have been told to remove a statement on a slide or not bring something up. Total bullshit. I should have said something as a drill sergeant, and I would always say something going forward.

Years later, on my second deployment to Iraq, I ran into an old drill sergeant buddy who told me Jason Bishop had died a hero while saving his brigade commander in battle. SFC Bishop was serving as a personal security detachment (PSD) for the brigade commander, who was famous for his role in *Black Hawk Down*. Colonel (COL) "Hooah" and his team were driving down a road in Iraq with Bishop's crew as rear security. Bishop's crew spotted a vehicle slam on its brakes, do a 180-degree turn, and accelerate toward them.

On 01 January 2006, SFC Jason L. Bishop selflessly blocked the road with his vehicle. He engaged the enemy, and they detonated the vehicle-borne improvised explosive device (VBIED), or car bomb. SFC Bishop was killed instantly while saving the lives of his platoon and leadership. I will see you in Valhalla, my friend, and recount the fun times we had together.

CHAPTER 8

ANOTHER WHOREHOUSE STORY

I apologize for the story you are about to read. In the previous prostitute story, I was a young sergeant. Unfortunately, this time, I was a seasoned sergeant first class (SFC) and considered a senior noncommissioned officer. I would like to think I promoted better values in my soldiers, but I didn't reach all of them.

In 2002, I was fortunate to finish my time as a drill sergeant unscathed, and was very proud of the cavalry scouts we produced during my two years on the trail.

When people came off the trail (nickname for your tour of duty), our cavalry branch was excellent at helping with the next assignment. Generally, we decided between Ranger or Pathfinder School, with our choice of duty station after. My wife and son had returned to Germany ahead of me because her three years off—for motherhood—were up. My wife is German, so I had a lot of incentive to return.

When my branch manager gave me the option of schools, I immediately chose Ranger School. Although I was a little out of shape, having grown lazy at the tail end of my stint as a drill sergeant, I could still pass. It would only be a physical challenge for me, not mental or technical.

"I can slot you for Ranger School, brother, and then send you to Fort Bragg [Airborne], Fort Carson, or Fort Hood."

"How do I get to Germany, Sergeant?" I asked.

"Don't go to Ranger School. Go to Pathfinder School with follow-on to Germany" was his response.

So, Pathfinder School it was. I don't regret the decision; one of my goals was to finish Ranger School, but family came first this time. I typically sacrificed my family for the Army, but in this case, I couldn't.

Pathfinder School was one of the most mentally challenging courses I have been to, but I passed with flying colors and jumped on a plane to Germany. When I arrived, I was told I was being sent back to Friedberg, Germany. I had previously spent six years in Friedberg. This time I was going to be part of a new formation called a brigade reconnaissance troop (BRT), which would be the eyes and ears for an armored (heavy tank) brigade of about 5,000 soldiers.

I reported for duty and was assigned to 1st Platoon, call sign "Red Platoon." Three of my soldiers had been my privates as a drill sergeant, so I'm sure they shit their pants when they saw me again. Over the next few months, we focused on honing our skills through gunnery, field training exercises, etc. Finally, we went to our evaluation exercise and absolutely destroyed the enemy. I have never seen one unit kick so much ass.

Our success came down to the soldiers and their immediate supervisors who carried the heavy load. Still, I must give credit to our commander, first sergeant, platoon leaders, and platoon sergeants. We pushed hard and led from the front in all we did. Our commander was seasoned, having commanded a tank company before this assignment, and was ranked as the best commander in the brigade. He was also a former 19D cavalry scout who took the opportunity to attend college and become an officer after achieving staff sergeant rank as an enlisted soldier. He was tough and highly competent.

Our commander also believed in always training, so we got along perfectly. He liked to call alerts out of the blue and go to the field. He believed our job was to be ready at all times, insisting that we keep our vehicles combat loaded (minus weapons and ammunition) in the motor pool.

One very early Monday morning, 0200 or 0300 hours, the phone rang at my house. It was an alert to go to the field. One hundred percent accountability by 0400 hours, order brief at 0500 hours, and roll out to the field by 0800 hours. We executed our alert roster (who calls who). Since I lived close to base, I shit, showered, and shaved so I would smell good for the field and started my drive in.

The vehicle drivers reported to the staff duty desk, signed for the keys to the vehicles, and went straight to the motor pool to begin emergency dispatch procedures. Gunners reported to the arms room, signed out all the vehicles' sensitive items (weapons, night vision, etc.), and began prepping to load them. Vehicle commanders and leaders went into mission planning. Very organized and sequenced. In the alert, they shared who had priority of effort, and this time it was Red Platoon, our platoon. We would be responsible for heading out before anyone else, conducting the reconnaissance, and establishing the base area of operations ahead of the main body.

I arrived at the headquarters, and everything was in motion as practiced. We gained 100 percent accountability, issued instructions, and off everyone went. About fifteen minutes before the mission brief, I heard the first sergeant yelling for me to get to the commander's office. I thought nothing of it. Maybe he just wanted an update to see how fast we could move after the mission brief; I was wrong.

"What do you know about such-and-such whorehouse?" demanded the commander. The second platoon sergeant, whom I admired deeply, was there as well—a deep-rooted military-family-and-traditions type of soldier, also extremely competent.

"Never heard of it, sir. I am married," I sarcastically replied, but I had really never heard of it.

"Well, Staff Sergeant Michaels from Second Platoon is apparently there, and I need you two to retrieve him!" he ordered.

I looked at my battle buddy and then the first sergeant, all of us wearing shit-eating grins because this might turn out to be fun.

"Roger that, sir."

We quickly exited the commander's office.

The platoon leaders would take the mission brief while my battle buddy and I found SSG Michaels. Again, prostitution was legal in Germany; however, it was understood that soldiers should not participate in that type of activity.

We asked around about where this whorehouse was. Astonishingly, most of my guys knew. They drew a strip map of how to get there, and off we drove. Thankfully it was only about thirty minutes away, so we had enough time to get there and back before heading to the field. My battle buddy and I had fun along the way, guessing what we would see and find. We were no angels, but we had never been in a whorehouse.

Unsurprisingly, the detailed strip map from our soldiers was spot on. It looked like a single, two-story house with a bigger-than-average parking lot. We exited the vehicle and made our way to the front door. It was about 0530 hours now, and we had to buzz the door to get it to unlock.

We entered a long hallway with a check-in counter about a third of the way down on the right. All of the doors were shut, and some chairs sat against the wall like a dentist's office waiting room.

I had likely been selected for this top-secret mission because I spoke German. An older lady—the madam of the house, we presumed—was at the counter and asked for fifty euros, which was the equivalent of fifty to fifty-five dollars at the time.

"We're not here for pleasure. We're looking for our friend."

My battle buddy described SSG Michaels, and the lady of the house said, "Aw, you mean Chris. Yes, he is here." (I'm using another made-up name for this story to protect his identity as he is now married with a beautiful daughter.)

"He is upstairs, my friends. Friends of Chris are always friends of mine. Go through the doors and up the stairs on the left with my Asian girls," the madam said with a smile.

Off we went. We were not expecting what we found when we opened the door at the end of the hallway.

We had entered another dimension—a vast living room with humongous, cathedral ceilings. A beautiful staircase in the middle led to rooms above. Couches, tables, and chairs were spread throughout like it was a spa. In one corner of the room was a buffet of drinks and fresh fruit for breakfast. In the other corner sat a mini weight set to work out on, and we saw an enclosed glass area with a small pool and hot tub. This place was the ultimate man cave. Lots of TVs and music played—*at 0600 hours in the morning*! To top it off, three or four men were lounging around wearing nothing but towels, with girls sitting beside them.

Trying not to stare because some of the women were completely naked, we hurried up the stairs and opened the doors one by one. On the second door, we found our "Chris" knocked out between two beautiful Asian women, who woke as we entered.

"Get your ass up and let's go, fuckstick. We're going to the field in two hours! You would be late for PT anyway, asshole. Get up!" screamed my battle buddy.

I was too busy laughing to see how mad my battle buddy really was, but I got the hint when he elbowed me in the gut. Needless to say, Chris jumped up and wrapped a towel around himself.

"Where are your clothes?" my battle buddy demanded.

"No one enters here with clothes. You go to the locker room, shower, and then change into a towel," answered Chris.

"We don't need the procedures; we need you dressed and ready to go," I half-heartedly ordered, still laughing.

We rushed downstairs, where Chris led us to the locker room, and he got dressed next to a German guy who came out of the shower holding hands with a prostitute, who then helped him dry off.

We left the locker room, popped into the hallway, and started to exit this not-so-upstanding establishment.

"Bye, Chris," said the old lady. "See you soon."

"No, you won't," my battle buddy replied firmly.

As we were leaving, I saw it: on the wall just before the exit was a certificate of appreciation. A certificate of appreciation is a military document printed on behalf of a command or unit and given to businesses, restaurants, etc., that support our soldiers. It is always signed by that unit's commander and senior enlisted leader; for us, that would be our captain and first sergeant.

This certificate on the wall caught my eye because it had our unit crest, which was a dead giveaway. I don't remember the exact words, but it read something like FOR MERITORIOUS SUPPORT OF OUR AMERICAN SOLDIERS AND THEIR NEEDS. YOUR PROFESSIONALISM, SKILLED TECHNIQUES, AND UTMOST CARE OF US HELPED MAINTAIN THE MORALE AND WELL-BEING OF OUR SOLDIERS. Etc, etc.

The certificate was signed YOUR GRATEFUL SOLDIER instead of the commander and first sergeant, and it had the whorehouse name in bold letters in the middle. It was professional looking and surrounded by similar certificates, unit coins, and patches.

"I'm taking this," I shouted as we marched out the door.

We jumped in my car and headed back to base, pulling up to the headquarters as the soldiers and vehicles were ready to depart. SSG Michaels jumped out and ran upstairs to get changed and ready.

My battle buddy and I agreed to wait to tell the commander about the certificate until the time was right, and that time was not now. We reported that we had secured the soldier and everyone was 100 percent accounted for.

My platoon departed for the mission, but before we left, I put the certificate in my desk drawer. The exercise went smoothly from there, and we returned after a few days. When we returned, we cleaned our weapons and vehicles and put everything away like the exercise had never happened.

Before being released for the weekend, our commander and first sergeant held a meeting, and the captain issued a new policy letter outlining off-limits establishments. Of course, the whorehouse was at the top of the list, along with many other establishments. While we were executing our missions during the exercise, the commander had quizzed all soldiers on every illegal or immoral establishment to help create the policy letter.

We never had an issue with a whorehouse again. As for the certificate, we waited until one of our dining-in ceremonies—typically an excuse to dress up, leave spouses and girlfriends at home, and get stupid drunk in the name of camaraderie. There are several official portions to the ceremony or event. During one such portion, my battle buddy and I presented our commander with the certificate of appreciation that he had unknowingly provided to a whorehouse. We all signed the back of the frame for him.

It was a great laugh overall, but I learned several lessons from it. First, accountability is essential; this would help me teach my leaders later when I served as a command sergeant major. When someone fails to show up to work, we don't simply wait and assume everything is okay. We find them. That is genuine care. Even if they merely overslept, always care for your soldiers.

The second lesson was about policy letters. Every stupid policy letter is written because soldiers messed up too many times. If everyone did the right thing, there would be no need to explain it in detail. From that moment forward, I scrutinized policy letters from a different perspective: What is the policy's actual purpose, and how will it be enforced? Is there a systemic issue that needs to be addressed—discipline, etc.—and how will you implement it if you write it? Sometimes commanders go crazy with policy letters and use them as punishment. Lastly, do you, as a leader and soldier, actually read and understand the policy letters?

CHAPTER 9

BANDIT RAID

I t was 2003, and I was a seasoned senior NCO with over three years as a sergeant first class, E-7. I settled into my platoon sergeant job in Germany and was done making stupid mistakes as a leader, or so I thought. Then, in spring 2003, our unit deployed to Iraq, smack dab in the middle of Baghdad.

After two months in Iraq, we were getting very comfortable with the Baghdad sectors and our job. The enemy wasn't using improvised explosive devices (IED) yet, so small arms, mortar attacks, and grenades were our most significant threats. Our brigade commander, COL Michael Tucker, allowed us to maneuver around the battlefield, and we enjoyed specialized operations with the multiple units in the sector. I was enjoying this first tour to Iraq, and the fear from the initial push north to Baghdad was wearing off.

One day, we got a call that one of the battalions, the Bandits, was about to receive a high-level mission, and they needed our help. We would conduct a high-value target (HVT) raid on a terrorist cell. This sounded very exciting. No need to ask twice; count us in.

Our platoon drove to Bandit Island in the northeast corner of Baghdad to meet the battalion commander and get the mission details. Bandit Island was a deserted amusement park with small roller coasters, dried-up swimming pools, etc. It had palm trees, and the area was vast enough for the tank battalion to occupy without too many issues.

When we arrived, the platoon leader and I went to the battalion tactical operations center (TOC), and met with the operations officer to get the details. With us were some special forces operators, some not American. The leader was a British Special Air Service (SAS) fella, who was pretty intimidating in size and stature. I'm 6'2" and generally have a decent build, but I looked small and weak compared to this guy.

The special operations team didn't have enough people to conduct the raid, so we would run the raid for them, secure the prisoners and house(s), and they would come in and grab all the intelligence, etc. When you combine different organizations, you call yourself a task force. Our company-sized task force would be led by a tank company commander whose tanks and soldiers were in support. He was a very skilled leader who had spent a lot of time fighting in Sadr City on the east side of Baghdad and punishing the enemy.

We formed several teams. Our platoon would be the inner cordon, responsible for securing the perimeter closest to the target houses and conducting the raid. The tank company would leave all but two of their tanks behind, drive close to the target houses but out of earshot, and set up an outer cordon, whose responsibility was to ensure no one came in or out of the operation area. To get to the target house, we would be dropped five kilometers from the site and infiltrate the rest of the way. Since we were just outside the city and in marshland, there weren't a lot of issues with sneaking around.

The SAS leader gave us a detailed description of the enemy and why we were raiding them. They estimated that approximately five to six terrorists and family would be in the house, so precision was necessary. The main house had a detached guesthouse behind it, closest to the water canal behind them. They had conducted a reconnaissance mission a few nights earlier and determined that the locks on the houses would have to be blown with explosives. This was getting interesting.

The special operations team had explosives experts there to walk us through door charges again since it had been a while since we had done that. Now I understood why we had been called in. We were masters of reconnaissance, so infiltration would not be problematic; we had conducted several raids already with a high success rate and knew about explosives. I was excited about this mission but needed to think about the dangers. That was why my platoon leader and I got along. I focused on the team assignments and the logistics side of this operation while my platoon leader focused on the threat. We blended our ideas and almost always devised a solid plan because we relied on each other's strengths.

We determined we needed more breach equipment to be safe, so I told my other scout section to head back to our headquarters, about thirty minutes away, and grab some of the gear. They quickly departed. We had about ten hours until the mission started, so we had plenty of time. We separated the platoon into subteams and went into our mission-planning cycle.

The team I had just sent back would be the lead reconnaissance team and lead our platoon to the target house. My platoon leader and his section would breach the guesthouse and secure the prisoners while my team provided security and prepared to engage any threat from the main house. Our field artillery platoon, a combat observation lasing team (COLT), would conduct the breach on the main house. They would split up into two teams like us.

The maps of the area weren't great—decent for mission planning, but we needed better. We had the battalion headquarters print off enough satellite photos to provide an excellent layout, and we began planning off the images, which were only a few days old.

In the middle of planning, my driver yelled for me and told me that my section had issues heading back to our location. They had *hit* a woman crossing the highway! I immediately got on the radio to receive the reports. Before you freak out, an official investigation was done after our mission, and no fault was found. The woman came running toward our vehicles, which were in the middle of a three-lane highway as they approached an overpass. The Army knew that the enemy liked to stand on overpasses and drop grenades on American vehicles, so we would enter and exit the tunnels using different lanes to confuse the enemy. Slowing down for the woman running toward my guys would have made it easier for the enemy to attack. She could have been asking for help or trying to warn them, but at this stage of the war, she should have known better. Honestly, the gunner should have shot her after a warning shot. Instead, he gave verbal and hand and arm signal commands to get her to stop, but she didn't.

The woman ran into the side of the HMMWV and got pulled under. The crew stopped, secured the area, attempted first aid on the woman, and called the headquarters of the unit who owned the sector to send their quick reaction force (QRF). QRF took over the scene. They were the right people to handle it because they knew the neighborhoods, people, and, more importantly, the town leadership to speak with.

Our scouts continued back to Bandit Island. The commander and crew of the involved vehicle were visibly shaken while reciting the incident details, and the platoon leader and I weighed the risks of taking them or leaving them behind. I talked with each team member and told them they did not have to go on the mission. We had enough soldiers to accomplish it without them. But they all wanted to remain on the mission, and we agreed.

In the blazing heat, we tried to nap under palm trees as we waited for darkness. About two hours before the mission execution window, the special operations team relayed that the enemy inside the house was now estimated to be around fifteen to twenty armed men, and they had plenty of weapons. This changed the mindset and mission parameters.

Generally, on an HVT raid, you are trying to capture one to two prominent leaders and their security. Until now, we had never conducted a raid with more than five enemy inside, so we had to revisit our plan to ensure we had enough manpower to accomplish the mission. It seemed we did, but our violence of action would be escalated, and if they were armed, shooting first before being shot was always a good course of action.

The time finally came. We were dropped off without incident, and our platoon began infiltrating the site. I led the platoon this time and put my staff sergeant, who had been in the vehicle incident, behind me. I learned quickly that navigating with satellite photos was not always a good idea, as the aspect ratio differs vastly from a map.

We worked through the trees and marsh until I spotted the canal in front of us. We had hit it way faster than I anticipated. Overall, the illumination was in our favor. It was dark enough to be invisible to the naked eye and perfect for night vision goggles, which we had. The only issue was that some of the houses had lights on because electricity was working in this area.

I gave the halt signal and whispered into our headset that we had reached one of the checkpoints. We turned right, stayed between the canal and the row of houses, and crept toward our target house. We reached the objective rally point (ORP) without being seen or detected and began our final movement to our positions. It was about 0200 hours, and everyone should have been fast asleep. We started a high crawl to our spots just to be safe. Finally, the sections reached their positions and were set up in a linear firing line about three to five feet apart from each other. The other team stayed by the guesthouse, crouched behind the wall.

Two dogs were outside the main house, but they hadn't detected us so far. The staff sergeant beside me pulled out his bayonet like he was Rambo about to attack the dogs if needed, but I just chalked it up to stupidity, and I remember laughing inside about it.

The COLT platoon reached their positions on the other side of the house. Our platoon leader then commanded the teams to prep the main doors' explosive charges. This involved inserting the blasting cap into the explosive charges. On the end of the blasting cap was the time fuse cord. We measured and cut the time fuse to give us a two-minute delay from when we ignited it, to provide enough time for the guys to get in a safe position. At the end of the time fuse was the fuse ignitor.

So far, so good, and the dogs were still quiet. After receiving confirmation that both teams were ready, the platoon leader signaled to place the charge, and they would sequence when they pulled the fuse ignitors. As our guy came around me and the corner of the guesthouse, the dogs became alert and started barking. Thankfully not in a panicked way—more curious. Our two soldiers placed their charges on the main house and the guesthouse door and waited for the countdown.

"Five, four, three, two, one, pull," the platoon leader whispered into the headset.

When you pull the fuse ignitor, if you get a distinct hissing sound and a puff of smoke, you know it's good to go. I heard the sound and prepared for the assault. Instead of sneaking back, which he should have since he had two minutes, SGT Stuart came running around the corner and smacked into the assault team stacked against the corner wall. He bounced off the lead assault member and right into the bush that separated the assault team and me.

We'd forgotten to have SGT Stuart drop his rucksack or assault pack when he set the charge, so we ended up with him stuck in a bush, and complicating matters was that his assault pack was now tangled. The first assault team member and I grabbed him and yanked him out. SGT Stuart got in position as the number three man on the assault team, and I quickly lay back down to assume my sectors of fire, just as the explosives went off.

BOOM, BOOM. The explosions were near-simultaneous, and it was beautiful. Ears ringing, the assault teams moved. We had put too much explosive on the guesthouse door, blowing the entire thing off the frame and making it easy for our teams to enter. Within seconds, our assault team had a man, woman, and child in custody and brought them around the corner to put behind the guesthouse.

Two terrorists came out the back door, one of them with a

weapon. The selector switch on my rifle went from safe to semi (semi-automatic), and I laid my sights on his forehead because there was an old car between him and me. I should have shot differently, but I aimed for his head.

It would be the first but definitely not the last time I squeezed my trigger with the intent to kill. I fired one shot and grazed the side of his head, and my SSG fired at the enemy on the left directly after. We both missed, but it worked out because the enemy dropped their weapons and raised their hands.

Meanwhile, inside the main house, we heard, "Room clear, room two clear," and so on. Within two minutes, they had everyone moving into the garden between the houses and then on their knees.

That's when we learned that Iraqi walls are made differently than American or European walls.

"You guys almost shot me," said one COLT leader. The tracer round I had fired—the first round to guide everyone to where I was shooting—nicked my target, traveled through two walls, and passed the other assault team. That near miss made us rethink where and how we positioned people for future raids.

With the site secured and the inner cordon set, we brought in the special operations team, who conducted their sensitive site exploitation. We also came across a room about ten by twelve feet, similar to a standard bedroom, that was filled with big black trash bags. Each trash bag was stuffed to the brim with American hundred-dollar bills.

Thank God they didn't ask me to count the money or secure the bags. I don't know how far my Army values would have held up if left alone—just kidding! But it was the most money I would ever see in my lifetime.

We secured nine terrorists, three HVTs, and a crap load of weapons to boot. It was an extremely successful mission. After returning to Bandit Island, the special operations team came by and shook every one of our soldiers' hands and said that it was one of the best-executed raids they had ever seen. It would also lead to many more dangerous missions, but we had the confidence and experience to execute them all.

The biggest lesson I learned this time was about not missing my target when I shot. I will never forget that moment. I didn't regret trying to kill someone. I regretted missing, and I made sure my soldiers and I never missed again. When you only had three to five seconds to engage an enemy when ambushed, if you missed, they ran away. But if you hit them, they had to stay and fight, and we now owned the ambush and would kill the enemy. Ask any of the soldiers I led after this mission, and they will tell you the emphasis I put on marksmanship and shooting. We never missed again!

CHAPTER 10

CANTOR AND THE IED

Going to war is never fun, and I was scared. It would be my first time leading a large group of soldiers into combat. We were a great platoon and an even better troop when you put us all together, but I was their platoon sergeant, and I was responsible for them.

Our brigade owned the east side of Baghdad from the Tigris River to Sadr City. Our troop had a great mission, and our brigade commander laid it out perfectly when we were preparing in Kuwait: "Go find bad guys!" So our unit spent the first few weeks and months scouring Baghdad for bad guys.

We would call up an adjacent unit, tell them we were coming into their sector for a few days, and ask what they wanted us to do for them. Raids for high-value targets and reconnaissance missions were common. We knew the entire brigade sector within the first two months, and we became very good at what we did. Unfortunately, the good times would end soon.

Before deploying, all soldiers were given stop-loss orders, which meant no one could leave the unit or report to their next assignment. This continued for months while we waited for word of when we would deploy. Finally, two months after the Bandit raid, we learned that stop-loss orders were being lifted. Sadly, we would lose our beloved commander and our veteran soldiers. However, we would soon be receiving replacement soldiers.

Our now former brigade commander had loved us, cared for

us, and knew how to use us to our maximum capability to help the brigade. When our new brigade commander came, our mission immediately changed. We would now split up assignments. One platoon would escort the brigade command team around while the other conducted IED route-clearance missions around the headquarters. No more raids and finding bad guys. We became a taxi service and circled the headquarters looking for explosives. The only fun we had with these new missions was escorting the mail-run vehicles to division headquarters and back, and we thoroughly enjoyed the Burger King at Baghdad Airport.

But we did our jobs, as always, and made the best of it. I escorted the command sergeant major during escort duty, and my platoon leader, First Lieutenant (1LT) Troy Gordon, and his team accompanied the brigade commander. We began slowly saying goodbye to teammates rotating out of the theater and welcoming new soldiers. One of those soldiers was PVT David Cantor from California. He was assigned to my platoon, and we made him one of our drivers.

Cantor was of Colombian descent and grew up on California's not-so-lovely streets. He had a chip on his shoulder but did what was asked and was eager to learn. One of his first missions was with me on circle-the-headquarters route-clearance duty.

One morning, we drove to the 501st Battalion headquarters forward operations base (FOB) because they had the best breakfasts in the area. We finished eating and started our first IED sweep before the sun rose too high. It averaged about 110 degrees Fahrenheit, but when you added on city heat with pavement and buildings, no shade, and fifty pounds of gear, it sucked ass. We would typically go out for a two-hour mission, come back, change our uniforms, hang up the sweat-soaked ones, and go back out. Repeat every few hours.

We started the clearance mission and immediately found a suspected IED near the underpass by our brigade headquarters. We had done this mission so often that we knew when things were out of place, and something seemed off. The ground had been recently disturbed near one of the overpass pillars, where many vehicles were required to turn toward our headquarters from one of our main routes.

The lead vehicle spotted it. After executing our battle drill for a suspected IED, I confirmed that it was one, and our teams established blocking positions a safe distance away so the locals would not be injured and no one would enter the area. We also started visual sweeps for secondary IEDs. The enemy had learned our drills from watching us and would often place an obvious IED for us to spot with a little effort but hide bigger and more dangerous explosives where they thought we would establish our blocking positions. So we also cleared those areas, sent the reports to our higher headquarters, and requested that explosive ordnance detachment (EOD) personnel come out to take a look.

Now, this is vastly different from *The Hurt Locker*. In fact, that movie was painful to watch, and I hope that it did not win any awards for accuracy. EOD personnel don't run around solo and clear buildings by themselves. They are too valuable, and they specialize in neutralizing explosives. They are the best in the business.

EOD personnel must be escorted everywhere by another element to protect them. They are also in high demand, and we needed more of them to go around. So, we had to sit in the heat and wait and wait and wait. One of my sergeants even asked if we could throw a grenade at it or shoot it. The answer was no.

The great thing about having EOD take care of IEDs was that they could determine the trigger method. For example, was it remote detonated by someone nearby using a cell phone? Was it command detonated with a wire attached to a firing device wielded by someone hiding?

EOD finally showed up with their escorts, and we guided them to safe blocking positions. They got out, approached me, and I locked them on the target ahead of us. Using binoculars, they spotted the IED and determined that it was a pretty dangerous one. EOD was using a new technique: they would use a water charge instead of explosives. The water charge would blow up and separate the explosives from the trigger mechanism, and they could recover everything instead of making a massive hole in the ground. Since this was near an overpass, that seemed like a good idea.

EOD unloaded their robot and got it ready to bring the water charge to the IED. The person operating the robot was extremely good at what he did, and the robot quickly made it to the IED. Through my binoculars, I watched the robot set the charge up and get it ready.

As the robot backed away to turn around, either it got stuck or the transmitter stopped working. We watched and waited. I finally got impatient and asked the lead EOD soldier about the matter.

"The robot is stuck. We need to go down there and get it."

Crap, here we go, I thought. I turned and saw the other EOD soldier putting on his bomb suit. I started calculating whether we needed to expand our perimeter to look for bad guys in case this was command detonated and someone was waiting for the EOD soldiers to get close enough.

I called the leaders over, and we mapped out two areas we would push to ensure no one was watching or waiting for us. I spotted PVT Cantor edging closer to us as we talked and decided to fuck with him, in combat, in a stressful situation. Welcome to the Army.

"Cantor, come here, Private. We need help. The robot is stuck, and we need you to go and get it," I ordered.

Cantor went ghost white, which was the reaction I expected. For someone with Colombian blood, he looked positively Caucasian at that moment. Cantor hadn't seen the soldier in the bomb suit yet. He looked at the robot, then at me, and very nervously said, "Roger that, Sergeant," and turned toward the robot. I was utterly amazed.

He didn't really know us yet, or trust us, and this was his first experience with an explosive device, yet he thought it was his duty to go down there, and that was what he planned to do. We immediately stopped him, of course, and laughed our asses off. You could see the blood rush back to Cantor's body, and a massive look of relief came over his face. It was a golden moment.

The bomb suit guy was ready to start walking when suddenly the robot responded—a relief for all of us. Once it was safely back, EOD exploded the water charge, separated the explosives from the firing device, and retrieved everything safely. Afterward, we actually dressed Cantor up in the EOD bomb suit, took a few pictures, and called it a day.

We had a good laugh over Cantor for quite a few days, but he took it with poise and quickly became part of our family. He was a soldier who wanted to serve, make a difference, and get away from the lousy path he would have been on had he stayed home. He made me proud that day and every day after—except when he tried to go AWOL on me a year later.

Between tours, we sent Cantor to Sniper School. Upon graduation, the soldiers needed to return to us immediately because we were in our certification exercise and getting ready to return to Iraq. However, when his teammates came back, there was no Cantor. He was in the wind.

Cantor had instead flown back to California, either because of a family issue that required his attention or because being in America was an easy avenue to visit family. Either way, I needed him to get back. I called him from the field, and he was scared and choking up while talking to me.

"I am so sorry, First Sergeant. I don't know what to do."

"I need you to come home, David. Get on a plane and get back to us, and we'll work everything out," I calmly stated, and I meant every word of it.

A few days later, he returned. We ripped his rank off and demoted him to private, but if you check the official paperwork, there won't be anything on the incident, and as far as everyone knew, the punishment had been served.

David was an exceptional soldier who made a mistake, but we understood why, and he was our family. Years later, David got out of the Army, met a beautiful woman, and asked me to be a part of his wedding. He stated I was like a father to him, and I keep those words close to my heart.

From the gangs and streets of California to a war hero and expert sniper. David has a wife, daughter, son, a master's degree, and was recently accepted into law school. You did alright, David, and I am proud of you—always and forever.

The real lesson learned here was soldiers have a terrible sense of humor no matter the circumstance. If you get shot and fall down and it turns out you're alright, your fellow soldiers will probably just say, "Good, because we didn't want to carry your fat ass." That's soldiers for you, and I loved every minute of being one. I also learned that soldiers will do incredible things for their brothers and sisters in arms, the unit, and their country. So never doubt the will and resolve of a soldier.

CHAPTER 11

THE FIRST TIME I WAS FIRED

First, I earned every punishment I am about to describe. No excuses. But there are multiple sides to every story, and this is mine. Some details I can't share in case statutory limits are still in play—and to protect the reputation of the worst commander I have ever served with.

"Fired" is such a strong word; thankfully, it's not on any official documents or evaluations I received. The Army is funny sometimes because we don't actually fire people; we simply remove them from a position and put them in another.

It was near the end of 2003, and we were about halfway done with our first tour in Iraq. Our first extremely beloved commander left; thankfully, his replacement was just as phenomenal. I truly loved how he treated his soldiers, and he was out the gate with us constantly, learning and seeing what we did. Unfortunately, he got some sort of disease and couldn't control his temperature and was evacuated back to Germany after only a month in command.

We were coming up on our third commander and were only halfway done with our tour, which ended up getting extended, making it even worse. After a few weeks of our executive officer, CPT Brian Mack, running the show, we got word that a new commander had been selected. He arrived soon after, from leading a tank company in another battalion. That was a good start because we needed experienced commanders, and this position was supposed to be a second command for someone.

I rarely put any stock in first impressions in the Army. People try to say all the right things and are nice, but give it three to four weeks, and then you see the real deal. I always admired the leaders who came in and weren't afraid to rock the boat right away. Those were my people, unless they rocked something that I was passionate about.

The first few weeks flew by, and then the commander's gunner came to me and asked if I could pick him up some Burger King from the division headquarters since I had mail-run duty that day. I'm not trying to promote Burger King by mentioning them repeatedly, but they were the only cool thing in Iraq at the time.

"Why don't you guys come with us? Tell the commander to get off his ass and join us," I said sarcastically.

"We don't go out the gate anymore," the gunner said, almost ashamed.

I then realized that my joke was actually the truth. I had never seen the commander leave the gate. I asked the gunner when they had last done so, and he couldn't remember. So, I did the noble thing and picked them up some Whoppers, which they happily ate cold when we returned.

In early October, our platoon was conducting vehicle maintenance in our PT uniforms when we heard the call on the radio from 2nd Platoon.

"Contact, IED, tunnel west, out!" reported the platoon sergeant. "We need quick reaction force ASAP, multiple wounded."

Without hesitation, our guys threw on our gear and sped out the gate toward them. There was only one tunnel in the brigade headquarters footprint, and it was near the Green Zone and the Tigris river. We were one to two kilometers away and reached them very quickly.

Second Platoon had the scene under control but was treating casualties, securing the area, and looking for the enemy who had laid the IED attack. I offered to grab the wounded and head just over the bridge to the Green Zone and the hospital. The gunner, Heath Hughes, had a a massive gash on his forehead, and I was looking at his skull as they began to bandage him. The rest of the crew was generally alright with superficial wounds but needed to get checked out. So, we grabbed the wounded and headed for the Kahn Bani Sad hospital while the other half of our platoon stayed back to support 2nd Platoon.

We were at the hospital for several hours, and the hospital was only ten minutes or so from our base. Want to know who never showed up to see his wounded men? Want to know who never went out the gate to the point of friction? You guessed it! Absolute nonsense, and something we were about to talk about. We eventually got back, and the soldiers were told they were day-to-day, but the gunner, Heath Hughes, was really messed up and suffered for many months and years after this.

The next day, we gathered as leaders to conduct an after-action review (AAR). This is where we see what happened, how everyone reacted, and what could be done differently, the same, or better next time. But, again, I was adamant about the issue of leadership not being with the soldiers, and I was overly candid with my command team, specifically my commander. Our executive officer, CPT Mack, agreed and helped push the issue. CPT Mack was well respected, and most of us wished they had just named him the commander since he led us with ease.

The command team had no excuses and knew they were wrong. We all agreed that the commander and first sergeant need to assess the situation, and if their *entire* troop was in contact, that was where they should probably be. The executive officer could control the tactical operations center (TOC) if necessary.

Precisely two days later, on the seventeenth of October 2003, while escorting the brigade command sergeant major back from Bandit Island, my vehicle was attacked with an IED. We were the lead vehicle in the attack, and our gunner started screaming, "I'm hit; I can't see." Despite being wounded, the driver did the right thing and got us as far out of the possible ambush site as he could before the HMMWV died. I grabbed the gunner and yanked him down from the hatch to assess him. My left side was stinging, but that was not my concern.

We would all be okay, but the HMMWV took extensive damage. All four tires were blown, and the windows and left side of the HMMWV was peppered with pellets. Thankfully, the IED was not sophisticated—basically a grape charge, an explosive made out of a can packed with explosives, packing material, nails, etc. The enemy had placed the explosive like a shape or directional charge toward their target, which was us.

The vehicles behind me did their jobs scanning for the enemy, looking for additional explosives or ambush attack points, and coming to check on us. One of our two radios was destroyed, but I was able to call in the contact and spot reports to our headquarters.

The rest of my platoon, led by 1LT Troy Gordon, and all of 2nd Platoon was spun up and heading our way. We told them what route to take because the highway was divided by a canal; they needed to drive up the opposite side of Route Pluto to reach us. Meanwhile, at the IED site, the medic and the brigade command sergeant major, Eric Cooke, ran to us immediately after the explosion, treated us, and helped assess the damage to the vehicle.

First Lieutenant Gordon and 2nd Platoon reached us quickly, and we all prepared my HMMWV to be towed back. As we were about to depart, our commander finally showed up with our XO. CPT Mack had a concerned look on his face but was also very upset.

"What's going on, sir?" I asked as he gingerly grabbed my arm to inspect the bandages.

"Nothing, Sergeant. I apologize for getting here so late," CPT Mack replied.

We got back to our HQ and were ushered to the aid station where our physician assistant (PA) checked us out, made fun of our bandaging techniques, promptly fixed them, and gave us some warning signs to look out for in the coming days. Later that night and unable to sleep, I went outside to look at the stars and put some thoughts together.

First Lieutenant Gordon was coming to check on me anyway and saw me outside. We small talked for a little, and then he told me that the commander initially didn't want to go out the gate. It took all of CPT Mack's influence to force our commander to come to us.

How could a leader not go to his wounded soldiers? I swore then and there that I would never support this commander; thus began my downward slide toward being fired. Every time I looked at this man, I grew angry, and he knew it. What's more, he was using sleeping pills at night, so despite us operating the most dangerous missions at night, he would be fast asleep, leaving CPT Mack in charge most of the time. When I was disrespectful with my comments or asked our commander if he wanted to come on a mission with us, I knew he was making mental notes to get rid of me.

My platoon responded when a big explosion went off just across from our headquarters but technically out of our sector by 100 meters. Despite pulling people from a burning building and running with a decapitated body, which I didn't realize until I got out of the building, I was verbally counseled for leaving the sector without permission. When I took our new NCO, SSG Damon Walker, on a foot patrol in-sector and we uncovered a huge terrorist cell, I was counseled for pushing the envelope because I told SSG Walker prior to the mission how we picked suspicious houses to inspect on patrol.

My days were numbered. Unfortunately, I let the "Chop that shit up" mentality outweigh my "Pay close attention to who you are pissing off" mentality, and I began to give him reasons to fire me. I also learned that I had torn my ACL and MCL from the previous IED attack and should have been evacuated, but I was not leaving my men.

Several months later, I had given him enough ammunition to get rid of me. Unfortunately for our commander, we were nearing the end of our twelve-month (original tour length) tour, and I had just been presented with the Bronze Star. On the back of the award recommendation, my brigade commander had written, ABSOLUTE BEST PLATOON SERGEANT IN THE BRIGADE.

Two days before we were supposed to go to Kuwait and end our twelve months in Iraq, we got extended another three months. We were sent to Najaf and Karbala to stop Sadr's army, which was rising up. An incident occurred during a mission where our commander acted cowardly under fire. Did I directly observe it? No. His gunner reported it to me, and I didn't let it lie. I reported it to the brigade command sergeant major the next time I saw him.

Meanwhile, I simply couldn't be in the same room as my commander anymore. Again, this was all my fault; I was letting him get to me. I was also putting my amazing platoon leader in an awkward position. But I genuinely believed the commander would get us all killed.

First Lieutenant Gordon was a soldier's leader, sometimes to the ire of myself. When we came back from missions, I would inspect our platoon's vehicles and weapons. Largely unhappy with the cleanliness or preparedness, I would search out the platoon, who was almost always playing Halo on the small TVs and game consoles in our living area. Right as I was about to chew their asses, 1LT Gordon would turn and just smile at me.

First Lieutenant Gordon was amazing and an absolute stellar leader in combat. He was decisive when needed, calm and collected when feasible, and led from the front in all aspects. He hated paperwork as much as me and wasn't one for drill and ceremony or pomp and circumstance. And he understood what I was going through, but I was tying his hands. When he told me to back off or stay away, I pushed our troop commander harder. I was stubborn, and I knew I was right. I can only imagine the pain he endured listening to our cowardly commander talk about me behind closed doors.

I fucked up after one mission and lost my cool when the operations center asked me to repeat my reports several times. I told them to fix their shit. I could talk to everyone in my platoon, adjacent platoon, and higher, but I couldn't talk to the headquarters. When I got back, the commander wasn't happy, and the image of him standing with his hands on his hips after we had just endured an RPG ambush set me down a road I could not recover from. I gave him a thousand reasons to fire me, and he did.

However, the brigade command sergeant major rescued me and told me, "Report to brigade S-3 staff position; I got this." He made sure my evaluation accurately reflected my performance. I had a Purple Heart, a Bronze Star, and an Army Commendation Medal. Additionally, I had refused to be evacuated after my injury. What could the cowardly commander do to me?

Well, he did the worst thing imaginable. They pulled me from my men three weeks before we redeployed. The men I had led for fourteen-plus months in combat without any losses. The men I had trained and loved as my own. I would have taken the court-martial over the punishment I got.

But I didn't get court-martialed, and I was put on brigade staff and sent to Kuwait to establish the wash rack for our redeployment. That sucked, but screw it; I was alive, and my men were too.

Upon redeployment, I had complete reconstructive surgery on my knee within thirty days of returning, and during recovery, my brigade command sergeant major called me.

"Sergeant Pinion, how long until you can walk again?"

"I don't know, Sergeant Major. They said running in six to nine months because of how severe it was," I responded.

"That is *not* what I asked!"

"Thirty to forty-five days, Sergeant Major."

"Good, congratulations, you made the master sergeant list, and I'm putting you back as the first sergeant in the brigade reconnaissance troop! We have initial reports we're going back to Iraq soon, and I need you back in your unit."

"Sergeant Major, this is amazing, but I am not returning with Captain Fucknut there." That is exactly what I said, and I laugh, even now, thinking about it.

"He has been removed. Get yourself better and ready."

If that wasn't motivation to recover, I don't know what is. Instead of thirty days of convalescent leave, I returned to brigade headquarters to get ready and show the sergeant major I was prepared to lead again. Within ninety days, I was frocked and sent back to the unit as their first sergeant—exactly where I was meant to be. Frocked is when you are on a promotion list, but your sequence number has yet to come up. They let you wear the higher rank and assume the higher responsibilities, but you are paid at your current rank until your sequence number comes up.

The funny part was that when the commander was replaced, he sat across from me in the brigade headquarters for the few remaining weeks I was there. One day he asked if I could issue him a computer he was supposed to have because I was signed for all the computers in the office. Of course, I told him to fly a fucking kite. That ended with me in the brigade operations officer's doorway, watching him tell me to get professional and issue the "worthless captain a fucking computer." It made me smile to know that people finally saw what I saw.

We must discuss this, though. What I did was wrong in many ways. I made it too personal. My shitty commander was an officer, and I needed to show him that respect. Unfortunately, someone messed up by allowing him to command, and he sucked at it, but he was still technically my commander. My career should have been over. I was fortunate, and my battlefield actions had a lot to do with that.

This experience reaffirmed what I already knew: my place was on the battlefield with my soldiers. I was a warrior and a leader, always leading from the front and not the sidelines. In a few short months, this leadership style would cause some of the worst personal pain and grief I have ever experienced in my life.

CHAPTER 12

T-BONE STEAKS FOR EVERYONE

It was February 2006, and our unit had returned to Iraq for another twelve-month scheduled tour that turned into fourteen, having just completed a fifteen-month tour the year before. We were a seasoned unit, and I was the first sergeant. We had spent the previous months preparing for our new mission, small-kill-team tactics, and would work with all the unconventional forces in-theater. It would be a fantastic deployment, but with costs too heavy to fathom.

Our mission changed as we sat in Kuwait, waiting to go north. Previously, we had answered directly to the brigade headquarters. There was normally a battalion headquarters between us, but we only had to answer to them when administrative stuff needed to be completed, like promotion boards, etc. Other than that, the troop commander and I sat at the grown-up table for meetings and events.

Now we were going back at the kid's table to be task organized under a battalion headquarters with the mission to do everything they said. We call this operational control (OPCON). There were no issues, as it was the tank battalion I had served in a few years prior. I loved the battalion, knew most of the first sergeants, and thought, in general, that the troop commander and I had an excellent reputation with the senior leadership. But apparently the battalion command sergeant major, Mark Schindler, didn't appreciate me being displayed like the "golden child" of our brigade and made sure I knew I was nobody special.

Although tough to initially deal with not being the golden children anymore, I understood later when I was a CSM, the importance of treating everyone equally and integrating new units together. Our leash just got shorter and in that moment, was not received well by us.

We began reporting to our new higher headquarters and received our mission to take over a small base camp occupied by an Iraqi Army unit. We would conduct missions all over the place, including the Syrian border, replacing a much bigger unit but maintaining the same area of responsibility. What we would not do was use our six-month training on small-kill-team operations.

We arrived at our new base camp. Dirt barriers surrounded it, with each unit (Iraqi and US) owning half. In the middle were two temporary but connected buildings, one for the Iraqi headquarters and one for ours. There were also towers manned by the Iraqis, a helipad, a dining tent, and tents for sleeping. A huge, loud generator powered the camp, and in the corner of the base stood a giant grain silo.

We settled in, transferred authority from the old unit to ours, and began conducting missions. The executive officer, CPT Jon Villasenor, and I immediately began camp assessments for living conditions, security, etc. We also briefed our commander, CPT Mike Bajema, and started putting our guards in the towers alongside the Iraqis. We wanted to show partnership and didn't quite trust their security measures yet. The Iraqi soldiers were improving but still had a long way to go, and we needed to figure out where their loyalties ran.

Our base camp was on the outskirts of Biaj, a town surrounded by colossal dirt berms that the previous unit engineers had built. There were four entrances into the town, north, south, east, and west. Each entry had an Iraqi checkpoint. With our berms and wire, our camp was only 200 to 300 meters from the edge of the town berm and houses.

Our concertina wire was held by pickets (poles) that we pounded into the ground. Well, the Iraqi villagers and, more importantly, the kids would come up to the edge of the base camp to steal the pickets. Who knows whether that was to test security or they were just being stupid? And the Iraqi soldiers would simply start spraying bullets at the kids from their AK-47s. This was why we wanted our soldiers with them—to handle it better.

We solved this in two ways. The first time the pilfering happened, CPT Bajema physically jumped over the wire and chased after the kids. Imagine your unit leader running across an open desert area, chasing kids who tried to steal from you. No protection, just him and the kids. Our soldiers caught up to CPT Bajema, who had by then captured two perpetrators.

CPT Bajema waited out in the open area for the town leader to show up, and then sat down and did a key leader engagement (KLE) with him and explained the consequences of continued action. We needed to build a relationship with the leader and townspeople. We were getting mortar attacks frequently and had to find out why.

Second, I built a shooting range between us and the town. We angled the range to parallel the town's edge by about 100 meters. The berm was not per safety regulations (deep enough) to support machine gun fire. As such, a few rounds could go through the berm and into the open area. Plus, we constantly shot, so whoever might be watching was bound to see tracer rounds pierce through the berm and into the empty space at some point. Anyone stupid enough to come from the town toward our base could run into some of those rounds. Stealing stopped, but back to the story.

Our corps command sergeant major (battle buddy to a three-star general, so very high up) was coming to visit our brigade headquarters, which was about one and a half hours away from us. Our brigade command sergeant major sent an email saying he wanted us there and included me in the email—just like if we were back at our duty station in Germany.

I responded that I would be there and started making plans with our supply, cooks, and CPT Villasenor to see what we needed while

I was at our brigade headquarters. We built the team that would accompany me. Well, the day before the event, I got an email from CSM Schindler:

> FIRST SERGEANT PINION, YOU ARE NOT SPECIAL, JUST ANOTHER FIRST SERGEANT IN THE BATTALION. NONE OF OUR FIRST SERGEANTS, INCLUDING YOU, ARE GOING TO THE DINNER WITH THE CORPS COMMAND SERGEANT MAJOR,
> CSM MARK SCHINDLER

This got me mad for several reasons: I did consider myself special, and I had made plans to get stuff done for my unit there; so I did the correct thing and played Mommy vs. Daddy games. I wrote the brigade command sergeant major and asked if he meant to include me because "I am under another unit now and told I am not special enough to go."

The issue cleared up very quickly.

"You are my BRT first sergeant, and I expect to see you here tomorrow. I need to talk to you about your future," the sergeant major clearly articulated. So, the case was closed, and I didn't bother telling CSM Schindler that he would see me at the dinner. Surprises were always pleasant.

The next day, we headed to the brigade headquarters and arrived shortly after lunch. I had my supply sergeant bring his big supply truck for this mission and gave everyone instructions to do their thing. I checked in with our S1 personnel services shop, grabbed the mail, talked to the soldiers, and ensured we were caught up on all our daily and weekly requirements.

Meanwhile, our maintenance guys scrounged around for extra parts to bring back while our supply NCO searched for any and all supplies he could find. Our team linked up around 1600 hours (4 p.m.) to huddle and share their findings.

My driver, CPL Regan Barr, said, "First Sergeant, I think I found a spot where we can get extra food." That was a brilliant discovery because we had not eaten well for the first two months there. Our cooks were doing their best, but it was one hot meal a day and MREs the rest of the time.

"Let's go," I commanded. So off we went, and we came to this big, bermed-in area with a bunch of refrigerator vans parked inside. We found an office inside, and I asked who was in charge and what we were allowed to take.

"You're here to pick up the food?" asked the soldier.

"Of course, that's what I just asked you."

"Roger, take what you need and let us know when you're done," said the soldier—who had just made a terrible mistake.

"Okay, boys, let's see what they have and load up what we need or can use."

We then went van by van and found all kinds of food. When we got to one of the refrigerators, we found it packed with T-bone steaks. *JACKPOT!*

To top it off, the soldier escorting us said, "We have to get rid of them soon, so take as many as you want."

This guy was my hero. Soldiers began loading as many steaks as possible in the back of our supply vehicle. I jumped on the radio to the tactical operations center back at our base camp.

"Fantom X-Ray, this is Fantom 7. Get the cook and the XO on the net ASAP," I radioed.

"Fantom 7, this is Fantom X-Ray. Roger, stand by."

The head cook and CPT Villasenor got on the line, and I asked them how many steaks our refrigerator van could hold. When the cook started to push back, I cut him off.

"XO, please coordinate with our local Kurdish workers and tell them to pick up charcoal. Sergeant [the cook], make room now and prepare to cook steaks for every meal until we run out. *Every meal*, and I want three hot meals a day, *please!*"

"Roger, over" was their response. End of conversation.

I signed whatever paperwork the guard gave me, and off we went. We then reported to the brigade mess tent, which had excellent, contracted hot prepared meals that looked terrific.

CSM Schindler was not the happiest person to see me when the time came. "You and I are going to have a very long, one-way conversation after this, so enjoy this while you can."

"Roger, Sergeant Major." But I didn't care because we had a ton of steaks in the back of our vehicles and would be eating like kings by tomorrow.

The meeting/dinner with the corps command sergeant major went well, and the brigade command sergeant major pulled me aside after and told me that he was considering making me an operations sergeant major in one of the battalions and asked my thoughts.

I told him I was honored and would do what was asked, but my soldiers needed me where I was. I was honest about it. I would always do what I was told, but I enjoyed being the first sergeant of this reconnaissance unit, and I had been there less than a year. Typically, you stay as a first sergeant for at least twenty-four to thirty-six months.

The dinner ended, and we rushed out of there to get back before the steaks went bad. Thankfully it was March, and we were in the mountains (yes, Iraq has mountains), so it was still cold at night. We got back to our base camp, and everyone had followed instructions. We had room to put all the steaks in the refrigerator, and the Kurdish workers already had charcoal.

I sat with the commander, executive officer, and mess sergeant, and we calculated how many meals we had to eat before the meat was bad or freezer burned. I was correct; we were about to eat three hot meals daily. I agreed to give him more soldiers since I had tripled his workload. I then set up a TV with a DVD player in our little mess tent and set the *Bring It On* movie to play on a never-ending loop.

For the following two weeks, everyone on our base camp shuffled through our kitchen, grabbed their steaks with eggs, and enjoyed a meal while watching a little *Bring It On*. Everyone eventually managed to see most of the film, ensuring that all of my soldiers displayed their "spirit fingers" while on the mission.

We were living like kings. Then CSM Schindler showed up one evening. He routinely visited his soldiers; plus we had a big mission coming up, and he planned to join us.

"First Sergeant Pinion, you realize you accidentally picked up a battalion's worth of food, right? And that you signed for enough food for a month, correct?"

Now, a tank battalion is about 750 to 850 soldiers, and here I was with about 100 to 125 soldiers.

"No, Sergeant Major, I did not know that. They told me I could have what I could carry, and that is what I did."

That didn't go over well, but at this point, most of the steaks were gone, and it was dinnertime, so we invited him to stay for dinner and to discuss the upcoming mission. CSM Schindler agreed and stayed there that night and three more nights. He and his crew went on multiple missions with us, and by the end of the third night, he and I were smoking cigars outside the TOC together.

"You are a good leader, Pinion, and I see why you are viewed so highly in the brigade," he said proudly. "Your soldiers are disciplined and execute the missions with expertise, and I am impressed with the cohesion. It's obvious that it is due to your leadership."

This caught me off guard.

"The brigade command sergeant major wants to put you as an operations sergeant major, which I believe he told you already. There are a lot of moving pieces right now, and other dominoes have to fall first, but when I get back tonight, I'm calling him to let him know I agree with and support his decision. You are exactly what we need in a battalion."

Now I was astonished and grateful for his comments. I reiterated that my place was with my men, but I would always do what was asked of me. With that, CSM Schindler and his soldiers left, and I am positive he finally understood why our unit was exceptional and what purpose we served in the brigade.

I did not end up taking the operations sergeant major position because we received a new mission. We were ordered to report to a city called Ar Ramadi, Iraq, and were about to do a lot of killing. Our unit required the team to stay together. It was one of the best nonselect decisions that ever happened to me. I was meant to stay with my men.

CSM Schindler and I are great friends now, and I genuinely respect him and what he did for his units and soldiers in his career. When I was selected for a general-officer-level position as a sergeant major, Mark was a civilian working in one of the sections under me. I routinely conversed with him to gain mentorship, but I always called him "Sergeant Major," no matter how many times he asked me to call him Mark.

Mark taught me it is necessary to visit your troops and units instead of evaluating them from the outside. Your direct sphere of influence is approximately three to five people; after that, influence diminishes the higher the numbers go. This is precisely why we organize as we do. First I ensured I knew my direct subordinates within that sphere, and then the tree grew with each level down.

CSM Schindler also showed me what a warrior looks and acts like in combat. He was at the point of friction every time and led from the front. He was technically and tactically proficient and was constantly learning and adapting as the enemy did the same. I learned how to be a professional and an expert in my craft from him, and he was instrumental in keeping me alive.

It is also important *not* to view conflict as a bad thing. Most of the time, something needs to be communicated better. Both parties ultimately want the same thing but sometimes take different paths. Understanding each other is important.

I also learned that steak is absolutely the best meal you can ever eat, in any circumstance!

CHAPTER 13

SOMETIMES THE ENEMY HAS A VOTE

It was July 2006, and our unit had been in Ar Ramadi, Iraq, for two months. Ramadi was voted the most dangerous city in the world that year, and our orders were clear: "Change that!"

I was still the first sergeant of this fifty-seven-man unit specializing in reconnaissance and small-kill-team tactics. Before the deployment, our brigade commander told CPT Bajema, our troop commander, and me that we needed to be prepared for sniper missions, ambushes, etc.

Our unit immediately began getting ready, which included sending soldiers to Sniper School, small-unit-designated marksmanship training, and cross-training with unconventional forces. We trained for approximately six months and had everyone certified when we deployed back to Iraq. Of course, as soon as we got there, we went to another sector up north and did our "normal," conventional tasks as scouts in an area that was quite boring, to be honest. We called it the terrorist training academy because it seemed like they kept blowing themselves up trying to learn about explosives. All that would change when we were ordered to Ramadi.

Even the movement to Ramadi was dangerous, with multiple IED attacks and stoppages along the routes. Our supply sergeant got confused during one IED stoppage and started following another convoy bypassing us. Granted, it was dark, and his vehicle had a man-portable radio for communications and no GPS tracking systems. Thankfully, we noticed him missing relatively quick, and my HMMWV was faster than his light medium tactical vehicle (LMTV).

Once we arrived at Camp Ramadi in June, everyone could tell we were not in the North anymore. Mortar attacks occurred daily, and we were located right against the enemy-held parts of the city. I said that correctly: the enemy controlled over 75 percent of the city, from government buildings to hospitals and neighborhoods. However, we held the edge of the east and west sides of the town.

The unit we were replacing never went into enemy territory, and it seemed like they had a gentlemen's agreement to stay out of each other's way. I will not name the unit, but that was the first time I saw a team basically give up in war. I'm sure I will get a lot of hate for saying that, but my unit shared my opinion. We had to force the unit we replaced to go out of the perimeter to show us the land. We call this a left-seat/right-seat ride. When you arrive, they show you everything, and you observe. You lead near the transition point; they watch and provide pointers to help you. Not in this case. The "tour of Ramadi" lasted about five minutes, and I didn't know HMMWVs could drive that fast. That was the last time we asked that unit for anything.

We had a transition of authority (TOA) scheduled around June 2006 from their brigade to ours. We would officially assume control of the operation, and they would go home. About two weeks before the TOA, CPT Bajema was reassigned to a tank company. This is a backward move for an officer. They do their initial command in the tank unit, and if they are the best of the best, they are selected to command the likes of us. However, for our brigade and the mission in Ramadi, this was one of the best decisions COL Sean MacFarland, the brigade commander, ever made. CPT Mike "Main Gun" Bajema had the perfect amount of arrogance, competence, courage, and audacity to do what needed to be done as a tank company commander.

The plan was set. The night of the TOA, our brigade would

attack the city. We would simply push from west and east and meet in the middle, no matter how long that took. Our unit was again attached to another battalion, and we were still serving conventional roles. But as a bonus, we would be in a close relationship with the SEAL team and begin planning for our small-kill-team operations.

For two months, we attacked the city and gained back control of approximately 80 percent. There was again a lot of house-to-house fighting, and when we seized enough area, we would build combat outposts (COPs) and place a unit there, right against the enemy strongholds. This method included limited artillery and air support to protect as much of the city as possible from damage. It was an infantry soldier fight, close-combat style, and our brigade became very good at it. We then repeated the process until another COP and area had been controlled.

One of our missions attached to this tank battalion was conducting route reconnaissance along the south side of Ramadi. We called one of those roads Route Gremlin. It was barely paved and skirted the edge of the city. It was also a main thoroughfare for the enemy to transport weapons and explosives from one town to another. Our mission was to stop the smuggling of these weapons and explosives.

We became adept at identifying choke points we could exploit, and we began setting up "snap" checkpoints to randomly search vehicles. We would hide and wait for one of our observation posts to relay that a vehicle was approaching. We would then pop out, block the road, and trap the vehicle in a location they could not escape. This threw a wrench in the enemy's plans as we put a severe dent into their operations. However, the enemy would not go down lightly.

One of the issues with traveling the same road is that patterns start to appear. The enemy began to reconsider how to attack us. This "evolving enemy" made life difficult, and IED attacks became the norm. One method to counter their attacks was to drive a different route for one to two hours, circle back, and go through the desert to our attack and observation positions.

While one platoon conducted operations with the SEALs (Task Force Bruiser), the other would be on reconnaissance duty around Route Gremlin. The brigade also pulled our 3rd Platoon, our field artillery specialists, back to their parent battalion. We needed more time and people to put total effort into one mission or the other.

Around the end of July, we started taking casualties from IED attacks. Thankfully no one was killed, but several were seriously injured, and the tension and stress were rising; we needed to rethink how we were doing business. We either needed to keep constant eyes on the route, which we didn't have enough manpower for, or ask for engineer route-clearance teams to clear the road ahead of us. Unfortunately, their priority was the city, and our requests for route clearance were denied.

One early morning, near the end of July, SSG Clint Storey's vehicle hit an anti-tank mine in the desert, immediately destroying his engine and HMMWV. Thankfully, no one from the crew was seriously injured. SSG Storey, call sign "White 2," was on crutches for a few days because his knees had hit the radio mount when the explosion went off.

The commander, CPT Dan Enslen, and I took turns with each platoon. He and I were in complete agreement; we would be with our soldiers and at the point of friction with them whenever possible. The platoons hated me going with them because bad stuff always happened when I was around. I don't know if it was bad luck or my keen eye for trouble, but they preferred the commander to accompany them on missions.

On 06 August 2006, 2nd Platoon was scheduled to go on Route Gremlin again. They requested a route-clearance team, and it was denied. I was scheduled to go on their mission, but the night before, I was told to be in a meeting with the brigade command sergeant major. Second Platoon conducted the early-morning inspections and headed out for their missions. First Platoon would replace 2nd Platoon in-sector.

After breakfast and checking on the status of 2nd Platoon, I walked to brigade headquarters for the meeting. The meeting wasn't really important enough to pull me away from the mission, but it required someone with enough knowledge of manning, personnel reporting, etc., which meant me.

Around 0800 hours, in the middle of the meeting, SGT Jared Rogers—our communications sergeant and the executive officer's gunner—practically knocked the door down to get to me. His eyes and expression said everything: something terrible happened, and I was needed.

We stormed out of the HQ, jumped in the XO's vehicle, and returned to our troop HQ. My crew had my vehicle ready, and our new medic was prepping everything in the back seat. SGT Rogers couldn't tell me what was going on as it was hard for him to talk and drive with his emotions going crazy, but once I got to our HQ, I heard that 2nd Platoon had hit an IED, and it was not good.

We jumped in our HMMWVs, and the commander and I took off. The point of contact was only five minutes away, and I saw the smoke billowing in the air. First Platoon, who was in sector already but farther out, turned around and headed to the point of contact as well.

Second Platoon had wrapped up their early-morning reconnaissance and snap-checkpoint mission and were heading back to base with SSG Storey and his crew as the rear vehicle in the convoy. His crew that day was SGT Bradley Beste as the driver, SPC Michael Hayes as the gunner, himself as the vehicle commander, and they had an Iraqi translator sitting behind Storey. Usually, the platoon sergeant would be in the rear vehicle, and the platoon leader would be in the middle; however, the platoon leader was on leave, so SFC Mike Olienyk served as platoon leader and moved to the middle.

SSG Storey's crew had just passed the Ramadi University walls and were starting down an S-shaped, curved embankment when the IED went off underneath them.

It was command wired, set off by an enemy watching from a nearby factory. It had been placed in a perfect choke point, on the only path down the embankment. You couldn't drive fast there, and if you were not careful, vehicles would bunch up. The ground was not freshly turned, so the IED had been in place for a while.

The commander and I made it there quickly with our two crews, and trying to figure out what was happening in the chaos was hard. As we approached the burning vehicle, I thought I was looking at the gunner's hatch. However, as the smoke cleared a little, I saw tires spinning. I was looking at the bottom of the HMMWV, where the IED had blasted through the undercarriage.

SSG Storey, SGT Beste, and the interpreter were killed instantly; there was absolutely no doubt in our minds. They did not suffer, but we could not get to them with the ammunition cooking off inside and the HMMWV engulfed in flames. CPT Enslen ordered 1st Platoon to head toward base and grab the base camp firetruck and force them out the gate to help us. This was a colossal no-no. They were civilians, and their mission was to serve the camp, not outside the wire. But those brave civilians defied orders and followed 1st Platoon out the gate to us.

SPC Michael Hayes was alive but hurt very bad. His leg was in shambles and on fire. He had to escape from the HMMWV. Trying to move, he realized his leg was cut in half and reached down amid the flames to grab the bottom portion of his left leg. Then, on his back, Mike crawled away from the heat. He made it approximately twenty feet before the first soldier reached him.

SPC Chris Buckley and SGT Regan Barr had been in the vehicle in front of White 2's and immediately stopped when they heard the explosion, jumping out and racing toward the vehicles. Chris heard Mike calling for help and went to him while Regan attempted to get the others out.

Chris immediately saw how calm Mike was, and they talked and laughed about wanting water. *Fuck it*, thought Chris, and he offered Mike water despite knowing how bad it would be for him. The others were dead, and the ammunition was going off, so Regan returned to Chris and Mike.

The heat was on their backs as Doc Herrud, the platoon medic, arrived and assessed Mike. SPC Buckley used his body to shield his team as they worked, standing between them and the ammunition. Mike's leg had been sheared off from the fragmentation of the IED, with only skin holding it on. He was severely burnt but conscious and calm. I am positive he was in shock but was aware of his surroundings and knew what was happening.

By the time we got closer, they had Mike loaded into SFC Olienyk's vehicle, and they raced toward my truck. We had practiced casualty evacuation and exchange several times. Typically, we would cross-load the casualty from one vehicle to mine. I would continue treatment and get them to safety while the platoon sergeant returned to the fight. But our standard operating procedure (SOP) was about to change.

As we pulled up door to door, I saw the anguish on SFC Olienyk's face. He was a strong soldier with outstanding leadership skills. We had been drill sergeants together years past, and he was a perfect role model for his soldiers. Easygoing, funny, and great to get along with. Today I saw the horrors of war in his eyes.

As we were about to exchange SPC Hayes from one vehicle to the next, Doc Herrud screamed, "Fuck no, don't move him." Doc was precisely correct. Mike was stabilized already, and there was no need to risk further injury. We adapted on the spot. I jumped out and then into SFC O's vehicle, and he jumped in mine; off we both went. This was possible because our vehicle's load plans, communication setup, and crews were interchangeable. This would become our future SOP on casualty evacuation.

As my new crew started back, I turned and inspected SPC Hayes. I held his hand and told him it would be okay. Since we were so close to base and 1st Platoon was on their way, I accepted the risk, and we traveled alone. I had to tell the driver, SPC Ruiz, to slow down a few times because we were bouncing around too much, and I didn't want to hurt Mike any more.

Mike was not in good shape as Doc tried to keep his lower leg attached. We made it to the gate in no time. I had alerted the field aid station we were en route and what to expect, so the medics and doctors were waiting for us at the aid station. I followed them in. The doctor told me to stay out, but he quickly learned that wasn't happening. I gave them all his information, blood type, injuries, etc. Meanwhile, the vehicle crew started cleaning the blood from the vehicle and getting it ready to return.

"Save him" was my order to the doctor.

"I will, but I can't save the leg."

I understood. The operating room was established, and the doctors wheeled Mike back as he closed his eyes from the sedation. Mike was and is a warrior and handled it better than anyone I know. His next battle would begin after being evacuated.

They took Mike back, amputated his leg, and tried to treat his burns while prepping him for transport out of the country. Meanwhile, the fire department extinguished the HMMWV and assisted with the recovery of our dead heroes. I stayed at the aid station and waited for the arrival of the bodies so I could go through the process of paperwork and identifying them. I am forever grateful to CPT Dan Enslen and SFC Mike Olienyk for keeping everyone back and helping the firefighters recover our soldiers, and I am so sorry for the horrors forever etched into those brave responders' brains.

When the bodies returned, the morgue did their underappreciated job of prepping them for their final flights home. I signed all paperwork and made one order very clear: "Everything goes back to America!" I was not leaving a single piece of American soldier in this country.

SPC Michael Hayes was air transported to safety and back to America for treatment. That night, we conducted our first angel ceremony for our fallen.

The transport helicopter arrived, and the morgue doors opened. Our unit lined up along the path from the morgue to the helipad. The rest of the brigade filled in after us. As each of our fallen heroes was carried out from the morgue, each soldier rendered and held their salute in complete silence.

After the solemn ceremony, we returned to the headquarters and began the process of assigning inventory officers to collect and store the casualties' personal items until we could ship them back home. We later learned to do this while the fallen soldiers' brothers- and sisters-in-arms were out. However, this time we had no choice.

Our XO, CPT Jon Villasenor, saw SFC O sitting alone after the inventory and collection. SFC Olienyk was rehashing the day's events and naturally questioning his decisions, even though they had used thermal imaging to check spots along the route and were cautious and deliberate in their execution. The XO sat next to SFC O, and after some small talk, he put his hands on Mike Olienyk's shoulder and simply said, "Sometimes the enemy gets a vote."

I will carry survivor's guilt until the day I join my comrades in Fiddler's Green. I was supposed to be on that mission, and I would have been the last vehicle. I say this from the bottom of my heart: I know there was a reason I was called to that meeting, but I should have died that day and not my soldiers. I would trade places with each of them in a heartbeat. I am content with what I accomplished in Iraq. Everything else is a bonus. If I could bring Brad or Clint back, I would. They deserved to raise or start a family. Mike Hayes deserves a life without constant pain.

Mike and I don't talk as often as we should, but we love each other deeply. He fought for years after his injuries to make an everyday life for himself. We need to do more for our heroes like Mike; we fail them profoundly in many respects. Our care for them has to be better.

Mike became famous on the amateur circuit for wrestling, and he asked one day what his signature move should be. Typical of Army humor, we wanted him to remove his leg and beat his opponent with it before pinning him.

To SPC Michael Hayes:

I miss you, Mike. You are my hero, brother. I love you and hope to visit your family one day and laugh with you again. We made a pact to open hot dog stands together in Florida, and I am holding you to it.

CHAPTER 14

GRENADES, RPGS, AND IEDS

We have to go slightly back in time to understand this story entirely. In April 2005, I was fortunate to be laterally appointed to first sergeant and take over our beloved brigade reconnaissance troop in Friedberg, Germany. It was a great honor and a huge responsibility. One of the reasons I was selected was our upcoming mission. After only a few months home from our fifteen-month tour, we were told we were going back for another twelve months. It turned into fourteen, but who's counting.

Our new brigade commander, COL Sean MacFarland, had a special mission in mind for us, and our brigade command sergeant major, Raymond Houston, made sure I would help lead them. Between Iraq tours, I worked in brigade staff after recovering from surgery to fix my knee from the IED explosion that stung me in October 2003.

Upon taking over responsibility for the BRT, I met my new driver, SPC Marquees Quick. SPC Quick was a brilliant young soldier from Hoover, Alabama, who was a wizard with computers. Within one week, I realized SPC Quick was the go-to man in the unit. As my driver, he was also the administrative or personnel services soldier and would process paperwork from awards, leave requests, promotion packets—all the basic office paperwork bullshit.

I saw the soldiers' actual leaders weren't taking care of their own soldiers because Quick was doing their jobs for them. So, after one week on the job, I told my commander that Quick needed to be moved back into a scout platoon.

"You can't do that, First Sergeant. Quick is vital to our troop's success," the captain protested.

"I am doing it, sir, right after gunnery coming up. That gives me time to look at other candidates and pick his replacement."

I knew SPC Quick needed to be an NCO and go back to being a scout. He was too comfortable and competent at his job, and it made the other leaders in the troop lazy. Besides, you only wanted soldiers working out of their MOS for twelve months, so I quickly found a new driver candidate, and the plan was in motion.

I kept Quick with me for gunnery, plus the new driver so Quick could teach him the ropes. After gunnery, I would move Quick to 2nd Platoon, where his platoon sergeant, SFC Olienyk, would finish rounding him out and prepare him to be a sergeant. As a side note, Quick's wife worked in our post finance office, so our soldiers never had a pay issue that wasn't resolved quickly. They were a dynamic team.

During gunnery, we were located on the farthest range from our life support area, so twice a day, we drove forty-five minutes to an hour to pick up chow for the soldiers. Lunch was MREs or Jimmy Dean's packaged meals. The three of us would head in, and I would check with HQ while the other two loaded the chow. Then one of them would take a quick shower since we didn't have water at the range—the benefits of working for the first sergeant—before we headed back out.

Some mornings I would let one of them sleep in, and once or twice they'd let me sleep in. That was how tight our unit was. They knew I trusted them to do the right thing, and every once in a while, they showed genuine care by taking care of me despite me acting mad on the outside for letting me sleep.

Returning to the range one evening, SPC Quick and I were alone. I must admit, he was the worst HMMWV driver I have ever had. Absolutely horrible. During the drive, he asked me what combat was like. He knew I had experienced several firefights, IEDs, and combat in general. I told him the truth about being scared on each mission as we went out the gate and happy when we returned. In between, you focused on your job and task so the fear stayed buried until the next mission.

"I am scared to die or let my soldiers down," Quick said.

"We are all, brother. We all are."

He was also nervous because most soldiers were veterans from the previous tour. I told him we trusted him and would be right there with him. Quick understood the responsibilities he was getting into.

After gunnery, we executed our plan and moved him into a gunner's position in 2nd Platoon. So, yes, I seemingly broke a crew after gunnery, for all the military graybeards out there, but I had SPC Quick shoot with the crew, knowing that one gunner was heading to another assignment and Quick would slip right in; technically, I never broke a crew.

Several months passed, and despite a dip in administrative stuff, we survived and soon excelled. Quick also excelled in his platoon and job. His soldiers truly admired him, and soon he was promoted to sergeant. We went through another gunnery where he shot distinguished (highest level), and we certified our tasks to return to Iraq.

As previously mentioned, our unit was in Ar Ramadi and deep into the fight with the enemy. In early August, we lost SSG Storey and SGT Beste and lost several more to wounds. It was a tough fight, and we were now fully engrossed in small-kill-team ambush missions. We were working and fighting alongside SEAL Team 3, Task Force Bruiser, and supporting our brigade and comrades.

First Tank Battalion, 37th Armor, was getting ready to attack further into the city, and we would support them. Between the SEALs and us, we would establish several kill-team ambushes and provide sniper cover for the dismounted forces fighting house-to-house. The battalion would seize and hold ground and then build another combat outpost. We had done this mission several times and knew what to do.

On the day of the mission, 2nd Platoon drove to one of the outposts, COP Grant, parked their vehicles, and waited for dark to insert into the sector known as the Second Officer's District. At approximately 0240 hours, they found a house, entered it, and secured the family in a downstairs bedroom, which was tactically the safest room in the house. Next, they went to the roof and began the painstaking procedure of drilling through the roof walls with chisels and hand drills (most houses have flat roofs with a three-to-five-foot wall surrounding the top).

Second Platoon identified two houses to support themselves and the tank battalion. We generally planned to be soft compromised within twelve hours, which meant people knocking on doors and looking for the family inside, and hard compromised within twenty-four hours, which meant an attack was imminent. People quickly realize when a family or kids have not come outside to play.

The platoons had to make a call. On a soft compromise, they could extract and start over with another house when it got dark or hole up and wait and see. During a hard compromise, extraction plans were made while we prepared for an enemy attack. Sometimes our best strategy was to take a house, design great defense plans, wait to get attacked, and simply kill the enemy. During this mission, the platoon had a soft compromise around the late morning after ten to twelve hours on-site.

Sergeants Quick, Barr, Wall, and Rodriguez-Dejesus were on the roof while SFC Olienyk, Doc Herrud, SPC Ruiz, and the interpreter were with the family downstairs. The platoon leader, in the supporting house, and SFC Olienyk began developing an extraction plan. The streets became eerily quiet—a tell-tale sign of bad stuff about to happen. SFC Olienyk had just radioed the plan to extract when four hand grenades came flying over the roof.

"Frag, frag, cover!" shouted SGT Barr as he dove for cover.

I have been involved in or near several grenade attacks, and you will *never* forget the sound a grenade makes as it hits the floor and explodes. *Tink, tink, tink, boom!*

SGT Rodriguez was "off gun" and asleep when the commands were shouted, but he quickly woke and curled up into a ball, as did SGT Wall. However, despite being the closest to the stairs and safety, SGT Quick moved toward the grenades.

SGT Barr screamed, "NO!!!"

Explosions rang out as the grenades detonated. Smoke and debris was everywhere as soldiers called out in pain. SGT Rodriguez was wounded in his lower back and shouting he could not feel his legs. SGT Wall, wounded in his leg, had already applied a tourniquet and began preparing for another attack. SGT Barr had been blown backwards during the blast and took shrapnel to his foot and buttocks (but would not realize it until he was back at the aid station).

SGT Barr assumed the machine gun position and swept the roof for any enemy or follow-on attacks. As Barr and Wall secured the roof, they saw SGT Quick unresponsive near the stairs. He had taken the brunt of the grenade explosions. Instead of jumping down the stairs to safety, SGT Quick had jumped toward the grenades to protect his soldiers.

On 19 August 2006, SGT Marquees Quick selflessly sacrificed himself to save the lives of his brothers-in-arms. There was absolutely no doubt in our minds. He was a true hero.

Doc Herrud and the platoon sergeant's driver, SPC Juan Ruiz, reached the stairs and began treating SGT Quick and the others. As SFC Olienyk came up the stairs to help, the doc, holding SGT Quick in his arms, nodded that he had not made it; Quick had sustained a fracture to his neck, killing him instantly. Doc Herrud moved to treat the rest of the wounded and prepare them for movement.

We sprang into action for the team's evacuation, and the tank company vehicles, assisted by infantry fighting vehicles, moved toward the house. It took a while to link the vehicles and our team up due to some navigation issues, but they made it to each other.

Unfortunately, not everyone could fit in the back of the fighting vehicles, so SFC Olienyk, SGT Barr and his painful foot, and Doc Herrud had to dismount and run next to the vehicles.

They were evacuated back to COP Grant, where they mounted their vehicles to head back to Camp Ramadi and the hospital. I was already at the field aid station waiting on them. The Bradley vehicle with SGT Quick in it continued directly back to Camp Ramadi, where I carefully helped unload Marquees, and he was pronounced dead.

The military doctor who pronounced the time of death was astonished to see the injuries. When I told him it was a complex grenade attack, he asked why Quick's injuries were on the front stomach area and not the back where someone would turn to protect themselves. One: Doc, shut the hell up; this wasn't the time. I was holding Marquees's hand while he pronounced him dead! Two: the injuries were on the front because SGT Marquees Quick, when faced with danger, chose to protect his soldiers and men above himself.

The rest of the platoon began navigating back to the main base camp and the field aid station, but their nightmare was not over yet. Along the route they were met by an RPG attack, immediately followed with a chain of three IEDs packed with explosives and gasoline. No idea how, but no additional injuries to the soldiers or damage to the vehicles occurred. All six vehicle gunners talked about the heat and flames as they continued driving.

Once Marquees was prepared for his journey home, the morgue personnel got me to identify the body. This was one of my worst and best memories because I got to say goodbye to my driver. It was beautiful and horrible at the same time. Finally, I officially identified Marquees, gently kissed his forehead, and said words that would remain between us.

When the rest of the platoon showed up, we hustled the other soldiers into the aid station. SGT Barr was still limping. He said he thought he had just twisted his ankle, but we started to see blood on his boot.

"Take your boot off," ordered a nearby medic. Grenade fragments had gone through his boot and into his foot, and also into his butt. Adrenaline, courage to help his brothers before himself, and probably some stubbornness allowed SGT Barr to perform all those heroic tasks despite being wounded.

I hugged him, and we softly cried for Quick and the others. He understood the pain I was in. Quick, Barr, and I had formed a special bond months earlier during gunnery—and in one day, I almost lost both of them.

SGT Rodriguez-Dejesus would be evacuated back to the States, while Sergeants Barr and Wall returned to duty within a few days. The next hard part was preparing for a memorial service. I was one of the speakers, and it was a packed house, with at least 300 people in our large tent. Everyone who knew Quick was there. Such an honor for them to come and say goodbye.

One part of a memorial service is the final roll call. Typically, you call a soldier's name.

"Sergeant Barr."

"Here, First Sergeant."

"Specialist Herrud."

"Here, First Sergeant."

"Sergeant Quick."

Silence and a pause.

"Sergeant Marquees Quick."

Nothing.

"Sergeant Marquees Antwon Quick."

Nothing is heard because the soldier has departed us and begun his journey to Valhalla and Fiddler's Green. Then you turn and salute as the firing party lets off a twenty-one-gun volley (seven rifles, three shots), and "Taps" is played. I never keep a dry eye during one of these, and my stomach still turns writing about it. It is gut-wrenching. Your heart is pulled from you.

SGT Quick is a hero, and I failed him. I failed to push to have him recognized; he should have received the Medal of Honor. I believe that in my heart and soul. We tried to resubmit the paperwork later, requesting an upgrade on his medal. Unfortunately, they required sworn eyewitness testimony that Marquees had jumped on the grenade. The soldiers could not confirm because they were diving for cover.

Alashia, your husband is a true hero, and he worshipped you. You two were perfect, and I am so sorry I couldn't protect him. Nevertheless, he saved lives that day, and although we failed to recognize him with the award he deserves, we know and will never forget.

I am sorry for failing you, Marquees. I love you, brother, and I look forward to smoking cigars and making fun of your huge-ass head soon enough. Take care of our soldiers up there. We will all be together again one day.

CHAPTER 15

HEISMAN

"The best day of David's life was the day that he died."

E verything I am about to write is from what I witnessed, heard, or was told by David E. Dietrich and his brothers-in-arms. Two news articles written about David back in his hometown said he shouldn't have gone to war or been in the military in the first place. I'm not agreeing or disagreeing with them or anyone; I simply wish to tell his story, which will haunt me for the rest of my life.

It was August 2006, and our unit was in Ar Ramadi, Iraq. Ramadi was extremely dangerous, as you learned in the previous stories. Our unit was helping to change that narrative, but we paid a steep price. We had lost three soldiers, one interpreter, and several wounded that required evacuation out of the country, all within two weeks in August. Our soldiers were tired and scared yet committed to the mission.

I faced the most challenging leadership dilemmas of my life and didn't have the answers. Looking back, I wish I had approached things differently. I became more complex and colder as a leader. I compartmentalized my feelings and emotions.

While holding an angel ceremony for my previous driver, our brigade commander, COL Sean MacFarland, asked me how he could help. "I need soldiers, sir" was all I could muster. He saw the pain in my voice and my eyes. I was barely holding on without breaking down. This conversation led me to meet and serve alongside one of the best humans I would ever meet, PVT David E. Dietrich from Marysville, Pennsylvania.

After the ceremony, we reached out to our rear detachment unit in Friedberg, Germany, and the conversation was candid and short: "Send us everyone you have." We heard rumors we were going to be extended beyond our twelve-month tour again, and Ramadi required our skills and our brigade.

"First Sergeant, what about Singleton?" asked CPT Dennis Wagner, the rear detachment commander.

"If he is medically allowed, send him," I ordered.

Singleton had been sent to us prior to deployment but was legally blind in his left eye. You can't be combat arms with vision issues like that. In their great wisdom, the Army medical board decided to reclassify him to become a truck driver. How could he be a good truck driver? Every soldier in a vehicle is responsible for scanning for the enemy, danger, etc. The driver checks his left side. You see the issue here.

That experiment lasted one day. When Singleton showed up for truck-driving school, 88M, they sent him back to us. So, he had sat on rear detachment until now.

"Send him, and I'll put him in the supply room here and make the supply room specialist one of our drivers or gunners."

We cross-trained everyone anyway. Not ideal, but it would work.

"First Sergeant, I would like to keep one soldier back, Private Dietrich, who just arrived," CPT Dennis Wagner said.

"Why, what's the issue?" I questioned.

"I can't put my finger on it, First Sergeant, but something is off."

"Send him and let us be the judge." I will forever doubt this decision. What would have been different for David had I listened?

They began the process of sending the replacement soldiers to us. A group of soldiers from basic training arrived in Friedberg with Dietrich, and they all passed their predeployment training without issue, including Dietrich.

Because of the dangers of flying during the day, all helicopters flew at night when possible. This included when bringing in the replacement soldiers. The helipad was only a few hundred meters from our tents, and our replacements arrived one evening in August. However, PVT Dietrich was not with them. When I asked where he was, the other privates stated that he had lost his Army combat helmet (ACH) in Kuwait, and they needed to issue him another one before sending him north.

We assigned the new soldiers to their platoons, and their leadership began integrating them. They were ready for missions within a few days, and the platoon leadership certified them as prepared for combat.

About a week later, PVT David Dietrich arrived. I didn't know why it took a week, and I had another conversation with rear detachment about Dietrich, but the details were forgotten.

The night Dietrich arrived, the radio operator woke me up and told me the new soldier was there. My first impression of Dietrich was solid. He looked like a running back with his strong, short stature and broad shoulders. He was obviously wide eyed, confused, and, I am sure, scared like all of us were when we first arrived in combat. I felt good about David until I asked him a question. It could be because CPT Wagner had put a bug in my ear, and maybe I had formulated an opinion already, but I immediately sensed something different.

While we were talking, it was as if I could see his mind trying to comprehend what I was saying. First, his eyes looked a little blank, then there would be an awkward silence, and then he would answer. Slowly.

Was it nerves? I've been told that I can have an intimidating stare and demeanor, and, again, I was withdrawing emotionally at the time. Plus, I was the senior enlisted person in our unit. Whatever the reason for his behavior, I didn't have a good feeling about it.

I assigned him to 1st Platoon, which was, like 2nd Platoon, full of rock stars. It was led by a very competent platoon leader, CPT John O'Hair VI, and a platoon sergeant, SFC Joseph Marco, whom I had mentored since he was a young soldier under me many years before. The meanest, hairiest, and most complex missions went to 1st Platoon. They would get PVT Dietrich ready.

After speaking with the troop commander, CPT Dan Enslen, the next morning, we decided to hold Dietrich back. I was thankful to have a commander who listened and trusted my advice. I told him I wanted Dietrich to be checked out by Behavioral Health. For good and bad, we had become very close with Behavioral Health over the last month, and we relied on them heavily for advice and guidance on our soldiers.

Dietrich would stay back from missions while 1st Platoon was gone and remain with the HQ section or me when I was not on a mission. When 1st Platoon returned, Dietrich went back with the platoon to learn more. Between us, we would train Dietrich until we thought he was ready. In concept, this was the same as we did with any other replacement soldier when they arrived, except that Dietrich's "onboarding" was a little more deliberate.

I asked Behavioral Health to run every test they could on Dietrich to ensure he was mentally fit and his cognitive skills were up to par. This took time. In the meantime, Dietrich became everyone's little brother and my personal helper.

This is what Dietrich shared about himself with me.

Dietrich grew up in Marysville, Pennsylvania, and had a hard life. He was abandoned by his mother at a young age and left on his grandparents' doorstep. I'm not sure he ever knew his father. For unknown reasons, his grandparents booted him out of the house in his teenage years, and he entered foster care. Unfortunately, foster care did not work out for David, and school was not easy either.

David left foster care around sixteen and lived in a car, at friends' houses, and at the local fire department. David enjoyed volunteering with the fire department, which gave him a sense of purpose in serving others. I asked David one day what it was like living in a car, finishing school, and trying to survive on his own.

"It was okay, First Sergeant. I got by. I used to volunteer to clean up the basketball gym after games so I could eat. I would pick up the half-empty popcorn bags and save them to eat later."

What a gut punch to learn about someone. David became like a son to me after that conversation. I took a more direct interest in his training and learning.

Behavioral Health came back and stated that David was fit for the military and they did not see any obstacles to his serving. They noted that he'd had assessments done in basic training, and those conclusions were the same as theirs. They did caution that he was a slow learner, but the method we used to teach him was appropriate.

They also mentioned that he'd explained how much this unit already meant to him and that he respected and loved me. That caught me off guard, but I understood why it was said. David was constantly complaining about staying back from missions to train, but he vowed to Behavioral Health that he would show us he was ready. This was around October or November.

From his arrival in August until mid to late December, David assisted me or the HQ section in raising the American flag on our little outpost within the camp each morning, he filled a lot of sandbags, and he trained.

"First Sergeant, how many more sandbags do I have to fill?" he would ask. Then one day, I finally showed him why. David was helping me develop a glass-house training area.

Think of a glass house as an architect's blueprint for a building. You see the lines on the paper and imagine them as the walls of a home. This was the same concept. We would lay engineer tape on the open area and arrange it like different house plans. We would then practice entering and clearing the buildings. I didn't have access to enough wood or plywood to actually build moveable walls to make visibility harder between rooms, but I could use sandbags, as tedious as it sounds, to replicate the structures.

David built the training site, and then we practiced clearing a house, with me showing him how to set up an observation point, sniper positions, and machine gun positions within the home. David became technically and tactically proficient in all areas between glass house, weapons, communications, tactics, and patrol training. Each week, we ran David through a series of tests. Then we met with his squad leader up to the commander to assess where he was and when he would be certified.

Everyone had fun with David. He became known as "Heisman" because of his love for football. David could talk about football for days if you let him, and he pulled the Heisman pose all the time.

David was a part of our family, knew his job, and regularly saw Behavioral Health for his mental strength training. By the middle of December, David seemed ready. We reran the tests. CPT Enslen was preparing to return to Germany for two weeks on much-deserved R&R (rest and recuperation). If David failed the tests, we would wait until CPT Enslen returned, but it ended up being unnecessary.

David passed with flying colors and was ready for missions. I will never regret that decision, no matter how much it hurts. Unfortunately, we received a brief for an upcoming mission that would make all of us question our previous decisions. We were about to dance with the devil.

We were a specialized unit within our brigade. This caused animosity among my peers because we were treated like the "golden children." Now, I'm not knocking on anyone. Those soldiers were in the fight twenty-four seven, every single day. They lived alongside the enemy in a city that wanted us dead and did everything to make that happen.

Anyway, if there was something another unit couldn't do, an area they wouldn't go in, or a sniper they couldn't kill, they called us. We were embedded with Asymmetric Warfare Group (AWG) personnel, who helped us develop small-kill-team tactics, sensitive-site-exploitation procedures, and mission analysis techniques. We partnered with the Navy SEAL team Task Force Bruiser and built lifelong friendships with them as we fought against the enemy.

The mission from COL MacFarland required us to go into an area that the Marines wouldn't and figure out where a famous enemy sniper was. The sniper would most likely target and kill US soldiers as they established the new combat outpost. Unfortunately, the Marine unit sectioned off part of the town with barriers, and there was no way in or out for vehicles. We were about to build another COP on this area's edge, the last hurdle of enemy territory before taking back control of the entire city. It had taken us almost six months of constant fighting to reach this point, and we were nearly done.

We immediately went into mission analysis regarding where the COP would be established. We used satellite imagery and talked with the Marine unit to develop lines of sight and visibility. Then we determined which target houses the enemy would use to attack the COP and which homes we could occupy to kill the sniper if he showed up. We had been chasing him for quite some time and knew his tactics well.

This was a complex mission. We had done some raids with the Marines and coordinated across boundaries and missions, but this time we would directly support them. Our tactics were different. Where we used stealth and reconnaissance, they used blunt force and numbers. Our small kill team was compromised of nine to twelve soldiers with teams mutually supporting each other. Their team consisted of around forty Marines in one house. This was something we would have to work through.

With the commander on well-deserved leave, the XO, CPT Jon Villasenor, would command and control the mission. The XO and I saw eye to eye on almost every issue or problem. When we first got to Iraq, he and I were roommates, spades partners, Jack Bauer fans, and I am pretty sure we were twins in a previous life. CPT Villasenor coordinated with all units involved while I focused on resupply and medical-evacuation procedures.

Since the teams were going to be dismounted, we adjusted our procedures in case someone got hurt. We couldn't drive to the point of injury, so we established multiple casualty collection points (CCP) around the area of operations. We switched out the standard stretchers (with poles) and issued the teams pole-less litters that would fit in their rucksacks.

We moved our troop to the Marine base camp and began our mission. Second Platoon infiltrated on the first night, under the cover of darkness, and conducted reconnaissance of all the houses, kill zones, etc., we wanted to use. Satellite imagery was good, but actual eyes on the ground were better, and 2nd Platoon was extremely good at reconnaissance. They bedded down for the day and extracted the next night. During the day, they passed all information to 1st Platoon, which was in the final stages of mission planning.

With 2nd Platoon out, 1st Platoon was the reaction force if something went sideways. I would be the lead evacuation platform and the Marines my escorts to the CCP. We'd rehearsed this several times on the map and terrain board with the Marines when we arrived at their base camp.

On 28 December 2006, 1st Platoon finished their checks and prepared to depart for their mission. They would infiltrate between 2300 hours (11 p.m.) and 0300 hours (3 a.m.) and establish their sniper team and overwatch positions. I was the last man standing on their way to leaving the compound. They filed by, and either a nod, smart-ass comment, or handshake greeted each soldier as they passed. Dietrich was near the end of the line, and his eye protection was all messed up—crooked on his head, ACH straps twisted.

I stopped him and told him, "Fix your shit, Dietrich."

He adjusted his eye pro and gave me the biggest smile I had ever seen from him. He was excited, and he was proud. He was a soldier! I reached out to slap him on the back as he passed, but he threw me a curveball and turned and hugged me. A big, strong bear hug. Ask any soldier when they last hugged their first sergeant like that. Most likely, the answer is never.

"I am proud of you, Dietrich. Listen to your NCOs and keep your eyes open."

"This is the happiest day of my life!" were the last words David E. Dietrich would ever say to me, and I still believe those words.

Once out on patrol, 1st Platoon established two small-kill-team positions overwatching where they thought the sniper would appear. Again, we got everything right about the mission planning. The houses we picked, the counter positions we found, etc. Everything was perfect until it wasn't.

Second Platoon returned from the battle handoff, cleaned weapons, prepared their trucks as the reaction force, and started to bed down around 0600 hours. I had just dozed off when I was violently shaken awake by the radio operator. Our XO was manning multiple radios at once and barking commands to 2nd Platoon and the Marines nearby. Someone had been hit in 1st Platoon, and they needed evacuation immediately.

On the morning of 29 December 2006, PFC David E. Dietrich had started his observation shift with his NCO and soon noticed something strange happening in one of the houses we'd identified. Dietrich alerted his team that someone was setting up a potato sack or mattress a few feet away from a window in one of the houses we thought the sniper would use. This is the exact technique used to mask the sound or sight of fire. Dietrich saw it and reported it. Unfortunately, the sniper saw him move, and when Dietrich repositioned himself to get a better look, he was shot.

Back at the Marine base, I jumped up and put on my boots as I gathered information. We slept in our clothes when on-mission like this, so it was only seconds before we were ready. I did not know who was hit or how bad it was. All I knew was the XO was pointing at the map and telling me to get there. I would get the rest as I was moved to the HMMWV.

My driver, SPC Matthew Clayton, had the truck ready and the

communications and GPS tracking systems booting up. Our truck was combat loaded at all times, and only two to three minutes after I tightened my boots, I was on the truck and good to go. However, despite being on call, the Marines escorts needed more time to prepare.

I'm not bashing the Marines, but what I'm writing is true. Their mission was casualty evacuation, and they were not ready, despite rehearsing this. This would lead to a near brawl about an hour later. I waited for them by the gate.

Back at the observation post, when Dietrich was hit, CPT O'Hair radioed SFC Marco to send the medic. He saw suspicious activity forming down the street. SFC Marco, in a supporting house position, ordered SSG Gonzalez and SPC Black, the medic, to sprint to Dietrich's house to provide first aid.

SFC Joseph Marco looked into their platoon sniper's eyes and said, "Cantor, I don't care if there are eight or eighty trying to kill us; open up a path and protect our soldiers as they move," and that is exactly what Cantor did as the enemy began establishing ambush positions on the street below. SSG Gonzo and Doc Black ran across the street, small arms fire erupted, and Cantor eliminated the threats as they appeared.

Gonzo and Black made it to the house and began immediate treatment on Dietrich. It was bad, but he was holding on, and Doc Black performed heroically that day to try to save David's life.

The teams saw enemy preparing for an attack on one of the houses, and CPT O'Hair and SFC Marco decided to pull both teams, since they were under heavy fire now and had no way to protect the dismounted evacuation movement to the CCP.

Back at base, the Marines finally showed up, and we flew out the gate. I jumped in as the last vehicle in convoy. At the same time, 2nd Platoon manned their vehicles and went over courses of action to support us and to close with and destroy the enemy sniper and ambush teams if necessary.

From the Marine base camp to the CCP was about two and a half kilometers (one and a half miles). From the CCP to 1st Platoon point of injury, in the overwatch house, was about 750 meters. The teams evacuated David, under fire and with complete kit on, for almost 800 meters. This was no easy task, and it was daytime. First Platoon made the right decision to pull the other team to help clear the path.

As we approached the CCP at a very high rate of speed, the Marines kept going right past the checkpoint. It was easy to see, and an American tank was sitting precisely at the intersection with its gun barrel pointing down the alley toward our soldiers, yet the Marines missed it. I yelled at Clayton to stop, and as the dust cleared, it was my vehicle and a tank at the intersection—no Marines.

I jumped out of the vehicle, ran to the barriers blocking the alley, and banged on the side of the tank. I wanted to see if it could push the concrete barrier out of the way and allow us to drive to our soldiers. At the same time, I heard gunfire down the alley and spotted green smoke billowing. This meant the teams were moving and using smoke grenades to cover intersections as they moved north toward me.

The tank never answered. I took off my combat helmet and banged on the tank hull, then finally gave up. I told Clayton to turn the HMMWV around to prepare to depart and told the gunner which direction to cover.

I saw the teams about 500 meters from me. I foolishly left my HHMWV by itself, next to a tank that never answered, and began running toward my soldiers. I reached the first intersection, and the teams were only a block away. So I popped a red smoke grenade and kept an eye west down a side alley for the enemy. The teams were taking fire as they crossed their last intersection before me.

SSG Gonzalez, one of the best combat-proven leaders I had ever seen, was the lead element in front of the evacuation team.

"They are shooting at you!!!" I screamed as he ran with four soldiers carrying Dietrich on the litter behind him.

"First Sergeant, you are getting shot at!" he screamed back as I realized rounds were hitting all around me. I had messed up again.

Focused on my soldiers running toward me, I stopped paying attention to my sector. I began to return fire upon realizing my stupidity.

The teams cleared their intersection and only had my intersection to go to. Just then, out of nowhere, a HMMWV pulled up to my corner and began unloading their machine gun into enemy positions. It was a fantastic sight, and to this day, we have no idea how they got to us.

The engineers had been building the COP when they heard and saw the firefight. They saw me popping smoke, and an NCO grabbed his crew and came to our rescue. We later recommended the crew for awards for valor to their command, but I didn't follow up on whether they received them.

With the machine gun raining fire down, the evacuation teams could cross behind them and to me. We tackled the last fifty to seventy-five meters to my vehicle and loaded Dietrich into the back seats, which were laid flat.

My medic checked for signs of life and continued working on Dietrich. Finally, I got into the HMMWV. Still no Marine escorts— just us. I was out of breath after lifting Dietrich into the HMMWV on a pole-less litter. The rest of 1st Platoon was closing on us fast, and the enemy threat was quickly diminishing.

"What do you want me to do?" asked Clayton.

"Do you know the way?" I asked, still trying to catch my breath.

"Yes."

"Then fucking go." And off we went, by ourselves, through the streets of Ramadi, with about three kilometers to the main camp and our medical teams. As we were leaving, 2nd Platoon showed up and was ordered to help 1st Platoon evacuate back to the base. If you've ever watched *Black Hawk Down* with the Rangers running out of the town at the movie's end, that is almost precisely what happened to 1st Platoon.

Second Platoon loaded as many soldiers as possible into their vehicles, put their vehicles on the edge of the road, and the rest of the 1st Platoon got in between them. Together they moved back to the Marine base—over two kilometers back, on foot, after fighting their way 750 meters under fire, and while treating one of their own.

As I gained my bearings and tried to help the medic treat Dietrich, the streets of Ramadi fell silent. We didn't speed because we didn't want to further damage him. We'd learned when we evacuated SPC Mike Hayes that speed is not always good. Stabilizing the injury and preventing further injury is equally important.

SPC Clayton got us to the back gate of Camp Ramadi. I had warned the base camp security we were coming with casualties, so the gate was open, and we flew past them to Charlie Med. Charlie Med is the medical unit, which provides higher levels of care and has surgeons to treat casualties.

We pulled up, and the medical teams took over getting David into the field hospital. I passed all the information along to the medics and doctors and got on the radio to update our XO and find out what was happening with the rest of the troop.

The platoons returned safely to the Marine base camp without further injury or firefight. However, we were pissed that the Marine escorts had messed up, and the Marine leadership was pissed that we didn't focus on the sniper once we identified his position. I was told that a fistfight brawl was about to start, and CPT Villasenor was about to whoop some serious ass. Thankfully, CPT O'Hair and SFC Marco were there to stop it.

Our XO gained his composure, and a call from brigade helped solidify the decision: our troop would return to the main base camp. I told them to pack up my crew's stuff, and I would be waiting for them.

I went back to the field aid station just as the doctor declared David dead. I had dealt with plenty of death and gruesome injuries, and the doctors and medics knew me well, but this hit hard.

The morgue is positioned beside Charlie Med for obvious reasons, and they transported David there. The morgue personnel would clean David up and prepare him for movement out of the country. Then I would be called in to identify the body and sign some paperwork. My crew had already alerted our troop headquarters, so they began collecting David's belongings for inventory and shipment while his brothers-in-arms were still out. I am not sure if this was the optimal procedure, but we'd learned previously it was the best way for our troop to deal with loss.

I had identified fallen soldiers before, but when the person came to get me, I physically couldn't raise myself off the bench outside the morgue. Right then, COL MacFarland—simply the best senior leader I have ever served under—approached and sat next to me.

"First Sergeant, take your time, but when ready, I need you to identify the body," the morgue assistant repeated.

"I can't. Please don't make me do this. I can't." I began to cry.

"Where do I sign?" said COL MacFarland. I will never be able to repay him for his leadership. He did what I no longer could.

My driver came to get me because Behavioral Health was coming to check on us. The platoons were returning, and I needed to be there for them. I remember looking at one counselor, simply muttering, "Dietrich," and leaving. I saw the color drain from the counselor's face at my words.

Once back at headquarters, we did what soldiers always do. We picked up the pieces and prepared for the next mission. But it sucked every time. We inventoried David's equipment and personal effects, assigned an inventory officer, and started an after-action review and 15-6 investigation into what had happened. Anytime someone is killed, enemy or friendly, we do an investigation. It is not punitive and should not be looked at that way.

The rear detachment was notified, and our personnel services kicked into high gear with insurance, arrangements, casualty assistance officer, etc. The first obstacle was Dietrich's life insurance. He wanted to leave all of his insurance money to his girlfriend. This was a no-no at the time, so the Army had to give the money to his family. Fuck them! His girlfriend should have gotten every dime.

Next was the actual family. I asked our rear detachment NCO to personally escort Dietrich home to his gravesite. I didn't want anyone outside of us doing it. They couldn't track down the family at first. When they located the mother, she couldn't afford decent clothes, so the Army gave her a voucher to purchase clothes for the funeral. They never found the father.

On the day of Dietrich's burial in Pennsylvania, our NCO reported that the father showed up barefoot and in plain clothes. The town was there, along with Dietrich's closest friends. Years later, a close friend of mine visited the gravesite and placed a football on his grave for me. To this day, I am mentally unable to visit the graves of our fallen, but I have vowed to complete it soon.

As I mentioned at the beginning of this story, months later, a news article said that Dietrich should never have joined the Army or seen combat. I will leave you to your own conclusions. I have many regrets and guilt, but I will always say one thing: the best day of PFC David E. Dietrich's life was the day he died. He died a hero, a son, a little brother, and our Heisman.

SFC Marco said it best: "It didn't matter, First Sergeant, who was on the window that day. The enemy was better, and he beat us."

I would like to share additional comments about his unit, the people who fought alongside him, and the proper thanks I never gave.

SPC Matthew Clayton, you were amazing, and I am so proud of you. I gave you shit the entire deployment and constantly pushed you, but you were a true hero that day. You should have been recognized with an award for valor and your Combat Action Badge, and I failed you, my friend. No one could have done what you did. You were brave, and I love you.

Doc Rob Black, there was nothing you could have done to save David, and yet, you did everything humanly possible to change the outcome. You kept David alive until we made it to the hospital. So many people need to learn how hard the Combat Medical Badge is to earn. It is the only combat badge that requires you to perform your duties under fire, and you did that. You would distinguish yourself that day and many more during our tour, and I love you.

First Platoon, you followed your extraordinary leaders, CPT O'Hair and SFC Marco, and you fought bravely that day. You cleared the streets of the enemy as they were forming an attack on you, and you evacuated your men under fire with precision and courage.

Engineer HMMWV crew, you saved us from further injury and stopped a possible ambush as we evacuated. You did your unit proud. Thank you.

Marines, we loved serving with you, and I proudly display my 1 and 2 MEF patches when the Army pisses me off. We both made mistakes that day, but we would fight with you again.

As you have seen through these stories, I made many mistakes in my career, but I am proud of the soldier David became. I should have done things differently, but hindsight doesn't save him.

I will see you in Valhalla, my friend, and drink with you in Fiddler's Green soon enough. And I'll let you order me to fill the same number of sandbags I made you fill.

CHAPTER 16

SHOULD HAVE BEEN FIRED, AND YEP, GOT FIRED THAT TIME FOR SURE

My "should have been fired" moment came after my second tour in Iraq, where I had basically spent almost twenty-eight out of thirty-six months in combat. Our unit was deactivated, and I was sent to the University of Connecticut to teach ROTC to college students who wanted to serve and commission as officers. It was an excellent assignment, and I loved teaching them. I treated them like officers, using "sir" and "ma'am" to address them.

But my mind did not return from war. I was in Iraq every second of the day and night. Pictures, thoughts, smells of Iraq and the men we lost haunted me. I was about to learn what post-traumatic stress disorder was, and I had it.

A year after arriving to the university, I was sent to Fort Lewis, Washington, for the Leader Development and Assessment Course (LDAC) to train and assess cadets. Everything was going great, and a Ranger buddy and I formed a quick friendship and were having a blast mentoring our platoon of cadets. Then we went to the woods for the final phase of assessments and ran into an absolute asshole of a soldier and leader.

He was technically the noncommissioned officer in charge (NCOIC) of the forward operating base where we were staying. He was the same rank as my Ranger buddy and me. He was horrible to the cadets, always screaming, a hands-on-the-hips type of leader. My anger was building fast.

The cadets had to draw M60 machine guns, the "Hog." Yes, you read that correctly: Vietnam-era machine guns that were replaced in the mid-1990s. So here we were in 2008, and we had to use them. Fortunately, my Ranger buddy and I had used them before, so we conducted the inspection and function checks. Unfortunately, half of the machine guns were broken and needed time to be fixed.

This cut into the time the cadets' were scheduled to test-fire the machine guns before going on missions. I continued to work on the weapons while my buddy went to calm down the NCOIC, who was being a dick to the cadets. Not long after, I heard my buddy raising his voice and saw the two of them getting into each other's faces.

I decided to calm everyone down and got in between them; it wasn't a Shaky Jake moment yet but was escalating fast. That wasn't a smart decision on my part because my anger was now like a short-fused firecracker.

"Let's calm down and stop being a dick to everyone, brother," I said, which I thought was calmly stated, but I guess not.

"Don't fucking call me your brother, and get the fuck out of my face. You don't like it, get the fuck off my FOB!" said the asshole.

Like my previous experience with my cowardly commander, I am unsure of what exactly happened next. I will say I earned another court-martial due to someone's hands around someone else's neck.

My Ranger buddy and I were asked to return to the main base, and I was sent to Behavioral Health, which ultimately saved my life. I filled out a questionnaire in the waiting room, which was all about doing drugs, abusing alcohol, and if I wanted to hurt myself. At the end of the questionnaire, I sat down and waited to see the psychologist.

The receptionist called me forward and said they were full for the day and that I had to come back in three days, but there were six or seven different prescriptions for me to take.

"I am not taking any medication without talking to a doctor. How the hell do you know what to prescribe me?!" I demanded.

"From your answers to the questions, sir," said the receptionist calmly and politely; but I wasn't having it.

"Get a doctor right now, or I will lose my shit!" I demanded.

A minute later, a psychologist took me back to her counseling room. After fifteen minutes of talking with me, she picked up the phone, spoke to someone on the other end, and said, "Cancel all my appointments for today and tomorrow." I am sorry for anyone who lost their appointment that day, but that phone call is why I am alive now.

I cried for the next few days. She listened, and we talked. She thoroughly explained what PTSD was. I was in terrible shape mentally, and the doctor saw my pain. I am not sure how many people have sought counseling, but did your psychologist ever cry from your stories? Mine did. She recommended in-patient treatment, but somehow, I convinced her not to send me and instead to help me schedule outpatient treatment back at my university. I was also told to stay with my Ranger buddy until the cadets left the FOB and went into the woods for their final assessment.

So, my buddy and I played golf for two straight days until we had sores on our hands from swinging the clubs so much. It was terrific, and I was able to relax a little. I didn't take the medication because I didn't want to depend on it without knowing more. I would need it a year later for my next assignment, but at that moment, I was okay.

I didn't get fired or in trouble. My senior leaders felt empathy and compassion for what I was going through. In fact, I think the incident was never reported, and to the asshole, I am very sorry for what I did to you on that FOB.

Skipping ahead, after LDAC, I returned to the university, where I was selected to attend the United States Army Sergeants Major Academy (USASMA). Upon graduation, I was hand-selected to transition the Germany-based 1st Armored Division to Fort Bliss, Texas.

From 2011 to 2013, while at Fort Bliss, I excelled as a division and battalion operations sergeant major, so the Army decided I was a perfect fit to serve as a command sergeant major. As a result, I was plucked away during the preparation for our upcoming Afghanistan deployment. I was fortunate to receive my number one pick of assignments, and in September 2013, I was sent to Fort Benning, Georgia, to lead a cavalry squadron of around 700 soldiers. It would be the highlight of my career—and lead to my "Yep, got fired for sure that time" moment.

When I arrived at Fort Benning, I was still not well physically or mentally, and for whatever reason, the doctors could not figure out what was happening to me. Without changing my diet or routine, I gained or lost thirty to forty pounds in a month. Most of you are probably thinking it was a thyroid issue, but nope, not it. Because of this condition, I had three different-sized uniforms, which was embarrassing in itself. In the latter part of my career, I was not the skinny guy anymore, but I should not have been that fat by myself.

And I should not have taken a command position with that appearance. I knew it, but I also knew what type of leader I was, and I had earned that position. Unfortunately, when I showed up, it was clear that I was being judged solely on my appearance and not who I was. Reporting early to the new assignment became a blessing in disguise, though.

Since I reported early, they had no job for me, so I hung around the brigade headquarters. Meanwhile, questions about my weight were already running rampant. In addition, my current brigade commander and command sergeant major were deployed to Kuwait with over half of the brigade, along with our division headquarters, so we just had a rear detachment of personnel and units who did not deploy.

It was quiet around town. I continued to see my doctors, attempting to figure out what was happening, and I timed my weigh-ins to match when a sudden drop in weight would occur. But, overall, I was not fit to lead a unit, and I shouldn't have.

Upon the pending return of our brigade leadership and unit, I was called into the brigade headquarters to have a meeting with CSM Tedd Washington, the division sergeant major, who was still in Afghanistan. I had heard CSM Washington was a bully from every sergeant major who worked for him. The virtual teleconference with CSM Washington was short and to the point.

"Sergeant Major Pinion, you are an embarrassment to the Army, and I have removed you from the command list. Any questions?"

"None, Sergeant Major." It was clear that he didn't care about me, my medical issues, or my history. As soon as the meeting was over, I called my command branch and asked them to get me out of this unit and to somewhere I could focus on myself. Within two days, I was out of the brigade and working for our armor branch on main post, where I could spend time figuring this out.

With the help of the post and Armor School command sergeants major, the military doctors reviewed my medical history and determined I was not at fault for my condition. Maybe it was the various drugs I was on for PTSD and other ailments—burn pit, Iraqi dust, etc.—but either way, I needed help, and they couldn't figure it out. Eventually, the Army doctors referred me to a civilian endocrinologist doctor. Meanwhile, I had enough paperwork to prove CSM Tedd Washington wrong and began the process of rectifying my career.

I reported to a civilian endocrinologist, who took some blood tests, waited for the results, and called me in a week later. I was bent over, given a shot in my ass, and told to return in two weeks. He had no bedside manner and never told me what was wrong, only that he was "trying something."

I felt great within a few days of the shot. My pants were not as tight, despite me not changing anything in my diet or exercise routine. I returned in two weeks and took another shot in the ass. Dr. "Bedside Manners" then explained that my testosterone was extraordinarily deficient and causing a metabolic imbalance. He had predicted that if he stabilized my testosterone level, it would stabilize everything else, and he was right.

I dropped weight in record fashion and felt good. I was sitting in post headquarters, not doing anything except working out three times a day and beginning to run for fun. I completed 5K, 10K, half marathons, and full marathons within three to four months. I was now in the best shape of my life; the Army agreed and said I needed to return to the command list.

For whatever reason, the guy who replaced me when I came off the command list was actually fired. I won't say why, but he also earned it. The command branch decided I needed to return to where I was scheduled to lead. This would go over as well as a fart in church, but orders were orders.

CSM Washington did everything in his power to not have me take a unit in his division, and quite frankly, he broke many rules and policies with his actions. He lost, but he made it painful by delaying the ceremony one month so he could personally attend it. It was the only ceremony he attended in my two years there.

The ceremony came, and it was glorious. It had been almost 365 days since I was originally scheduled to take the helm. Of course, it screwed the rest of my career and timeline, but I didn't care. I was leading one of the best organizations in the Army. Plus, the ceremony was attended by the post and Armor School command sergeants major, who wanted to see the face of CSM Tedd Washington when I received the unit's colors.

After the ceremony, I was called into the brigade command sergeant major's office, where CSM Washington was waiting. It was the first time I'd met him in person, and I still didn't like him.

"Nothing personal, Sergeant Major. This was business, and I am glad it worked out for you. I hope you learned a valuable lesson," he said from the couch while I was standing.

"It was very personal to me, Sergeant Major, and I learned plenty of leadership lessons from you and the command that I will take to my unit," I disrespectfully said.

"Care to share?" CSM Washington asked.

"Not really, Sergeant Major, but at any time did any of you ask if I was okay? None of you talked to my doctors or healthcare professionals. You saw a fat guy, and that was that."

"You are dismissed," said my brigade command sergeant major, who I think was protecting me or the division command sergeant major because I saw veins popping in CSM Washington's forehead.

I waited outside, too far to see or hear anything happening inside. Finally, after a time, the brigade command sergeant major found me and walked with me to my new squadron headquarters.

"You are starting off on the wrong foot, Sergeant Major, and Command Sergeant Major Washington made it clear to me that if I see you fucking up, you are done. Is that clear?"

"Crystal, Sergeant Major." And that was my welcome brief from my senior leader. This led me to run the squadron ragged the first few months, and I apologize to my first sergeants, leaders, and soldiers, but I wasn't going to fail them or myself, and I certainly wasn't going to prove CSM Tedd Washington correct; and I didn't. For the next two years, I was privileged to lead some of the best men and women I would ever serve with.

I share these stories, which are very personal to me, because they holistically show you who I was as a soldier. I was tough but fair, demanding, showed no fear to my enemy, genuinely cared for my soldiers, and did not back down from confrontations. But I was human, and I was suffering, and I needed help.

For the last fifteen years, I have attended counseling to understand and protect myself and others from my PTSD and traumatic brain injuries (TBI), which were discovered during some head scans. I was not perfect, but I did my best and did everything in my power to teach and love my soldiers.

I was basically fired two times, and one should have taken. But in the end, everything turned out exactly as it should for me.

EPILOGUE

I am unsure how to end this journey. I sit here today with tears streaming down my face as I finish this book. This project turned out differently than expected, and I am still determining what happens next.

The purpose of this book was initially to let others know about the heroes I served with while at the same time telling funny stories I experienced along the way; it was not meant to be a memoir. I am in my comfort zone when I think of all the good times and bad times I had with my soldiers. They were and will forever be what matters most to me.

But this book also turned out to be my therapy. It has been almost twelve years since I fired a weapon against an enemy and five years since I retired from the Army. Yet I struggle daily, mentally and physically, with the realities of war and losing soldiers.

For my retirement ceremony, my battle buddy BG Sean Bernabe asked for pictures of me to show as a slideshow. Instead, we only showed pics of my family and my soldiers, and it still brings happiness to my heart when I see those pictures or think of them. I have told only a few people about this, but my life is in extra innings right now; I am not meant to be alive, but here I am, still kicking somehow.

When I was leaving R&R and heading back to Iraq in 2006, I wrote letters to my wife, Solvig, and two boys, Damian and Tristan. I was saying goodbye because I believed I would never see them again. In the letters, I told Solvig to move on and find someone who would love the boys as much as me and asked her not to marry another soldier so they would have a dad that was around. I told Damian and Tristan how sorry I was that I couldn't be there to raise them.

On the way to the base, I told Damian, who was only seven, that he was the man of the house and to be brave and strong—to take care of Tristan, who was only one year old, and watch over their mama. I told him not to cry when I left because it was going to be okay.

When I got out of the car, I hugged my wife, who was sobbing, kissed Tristan, and knelt down to hug and kiss Damian, the man of the house now. Damian stayed brave and strong as his eyes watered and his lip quivered. I knew, selfishly, that if he cried, I might not get on the plane that day.

I stood and turned as tears flowed from my eyes, and I walked away, never looking back for fear I would stop in my tracks. I had just said goodbye to the three most precious people in my life. In that moment, I gave myself totally and fully to the Army and my men, knowing I was going to die in Iraq.

For whatever reason, I didn't die, and in some ways, I regret it. Not because I'm not thankful for what I have but because of the guilt of not bringing them all home alive while I got a second chance in life.

This book is my final salute to those I served with, and I hope I made them proud and told their stories with accuracy and honesty. I love everyone with whom I served, and I am forever grateful for the opportunity to serve my country. I hope someone shares more stories of our unit in Ramadi, Iraq, because there are many more details, and these soldiers deserve to have their stories told or shown on the screen. If you want more funny stories, I have plenty; these were just the tip of the iceberg.

Take care of your soldiers and loved ones, and they will take care of you. Everything else will take care of itself. Until then, roll up your fucking sleeves, and *chop that shit up*!

IF YOU AIN'T CAV, YOU AIN'T SHIT!

OUR HEROES

Killed in Action:

- ☆ SSG Clint J. Storey, died 04 August 2006, IED

- ☆ SGT Bradley H. Beste, died 04 August 2006, IED

- ☆ SGT Marquees A. Quick, died 19 August 2006, Grenade

- ☆ PFC David E. Dietrich, died 29 December 2006, Sniper

Wounded in Action:

- ☆ SGT Regan Barr, 2nd Platoon, Grenade

- ☆ SGT Hector Rodriguez-Dejesus, 2nd Platoon, Grenade

- ☆ SGT David Wall, 2nd Platoon, Grenade

- ☆ SGT Joshua Jones, 1st Platoon, Grenade

- ☆ PFC Tony Zanardo, 1st Platoon, Grenade

☆ PFC Robertson, 1st Platoon, IED

☆ SPC Matthew Wert, 1st Platoon, IED

☆ SSG Jesus Gonzalez, 1st Platoon, IED

☆ SPC Christopher Strickland, 1st Platoon, IED

☆ SSG Clint J. Storey, 2nd Platoon, IED

☆ SPC Michael Hayes, 2nd Platoon, IED

☆ SGT David Beyl, 1st Platoon, IED

☆ SFC Daniel Pinion, 1st Platoon, IED

☆ SPC Matthew Tooher, 2nd Platoon, IED

☆ SGT Jason Ellis, 2nd Platoon, IED

☆ SGT Anthony Bach, 1st Platoon, IED

☆ SPC Jesus Lugo, 1st Platoon, IED

☆ SPC Heath Hughes, 2nd Platoon, IED

☆ SPC Robert Ireland, 2nd Platoon IED

☆ SGT Bobby Shay, 2nd Platoon, PTSD

Lost Years Later

☆ SGT Jared W. Rogers, died 13 October 2021

☆ SPC Jose M. Diaz Jr., died 15 April 2018

SSG CLINT J. STOREY

27 FEBRUARY 1976–04 AUGUST 2006

S SG Clint J. Storey was from Enid, Oklahoma, and came to us a few months before our second deployment to Iraq. He served in the headquarters section for a while before moving down to 2nd Platoon during deployment. He loved playing poker and reciting every line from the movie *Joe Dirt*. After surviving his first IED explosion, he could have stayed back from missions longer but told his leadership he needed to be on-mission with his men.

Clint had a wife and daughter who stayed back in Massachusetts when Clint came to Germany. A few weeks before Clint's death, he went home for R&R. Upon his return and two weeks before his death, he happily told everyone under the sun that his wife was pregnant and was sure it was a boy. Clint's son, "CJ," would never meet his father in person, but Clint forever lives in his heart.

Fortunately, after Iraq, I was assigned to teach at the University of Connecticut, close to Mrs. Storey and her family. On CJ's first birthday, we were all invited, including the casualty assistance officer. We celebrated CJ, and we celebrated Clint. I sat with the entire family and told them to ask me any question, and I would answer candidly and honestly. No holds barred. It was a tough but necessary conversation, and I hope I helped them in some small way to start their healing process.

His military grave is at Enid Cemetery, Memorial ID 15168431.

SGT BRADLEY H. BESTE

23 OCTOBER 1983–04 AUGUST 2006

SGT Bradley H. Beste grew up in Naperville, Illinois, as part of a middle-class family and community. His dad worked in business, and his mom was a schoolteacher. Brad was the middle child of four and loved being part of a big family.

Like myself, Brad loved fishing, hiking, skiing, and outdoor activities like white water rafting. He honed his skills during his family's many trips in their pop-up trailer across the US and Canada.

With a last name like Beste, Brad wanted to excel in everything, including sports. He played baseball, soccer, basketball, and wrestled varsity in high school. Additionally, Brad wanted to serve his country and enlisted under the "delayed entry program" during his junior year in high school. After high school, Brad attended cavalry scout training at Fort Knox, Kentucky, and reported to F Troop, 1st Cavalry Regiment, 1st Brigade, 1st Armored Division, at Friedberg, Germany.

Brad was a standard bearer of excellence for 2nd Platoon. He was a veteran of our first tour in Iraq and actually had our first kill for the troop. He was quiet around outsiders, but you could see how special he was once he knew and trusted you. He liked to hang out with friends downtown in Friedberg and always wore his trademark fedora.

He was a tall, good-looking redhead who liked carrying big knives and decorating his combat crew helmet and was a master at his craft. Younger soldiers looked up to him, and he built close friendships with everyone in the troop. We deeply depended on Brad, and he is sorely missed.

Brad lived a lifetime. His military grave is at Abraham Lincoln National Cemetery, Section 10 in Elwood, Illinois.

SGT MARQUEES A. QUICK

17 SEPTEMBER 1977–19 AUGUST 2006

This was written by Marquees's wife:

Marquees Antwon Quick was born 17 September 1977, to Linda Rawlings and Mark Quick in New York. The family later relocated to Center Point, Alabama, where he attended Huffman High School, class of 1996. He was a family man who saw or called his mom and grandmom every day. Marquees was the oldest of three brothers: Matthew, Brandon, and Keith Quick.

Marquees joined the Army, but after his initial contract was over, Marquees left and joined the Alabama National Guard. When we first started dating, he said he never wanted to leave active duty, but personal issues led him to do so. We met at my church, which I was very active in, and I knew how special Marquees was when I witnessed him pulling people to the side and asking them not to swear in front of me. After 9/11, Marquees knew he could not sit on the sidelines and quickly transitioned back to active duty and selected Germany as his duty station of choice.

As my husband, Marquees was a great leader and motivator. He said a lot of the spouses coming to Germany couldn't pass the German driving test, but he would tell me, "I know you will pass it the first time. I know you can do it!" He brought the driving book home, and we studied for two or three weeks, and I passed. He was SOOO proud of me, and after a quick celebration, we worked on our next goal: a government job for myself. With Marquees's help and guidance, I accepted a position in finance for the post.

When he left for his first assignment to Iraq, I wanted to surprise him when he got back. When I got off work, I would do cardio and play basketball at the gym. The results really started showing! The unit family readiness group (FRG) thought I was depressed, but I was putting in the work to reach my goal before he came home on R&R. When Marquees returned, he didn't recognize me at the airport at first, but when he did, he picked me up and threw me over his shoulder; that was the best feeling ever!

We made an awesome team, and we laughed because we are both Virgos, so it was easy for us. He often joked that I was a cougar because I was two and a half weeks older than him. Marquees took his role as a leader to heart and never wanted to let his men down. He had a big heart, and he would say a big head too. Marquees was my best friend, husband, and cheerleader. The family misses you dearly, SGT Marquees A. Quick. Gone but never forgotten.

Love always, your wifey.

SGT Marquees A. Quick is buried at Zion Memorial Gardens, Birmingham, Alabama. Lot 9, Section 134A, Space C.

PFC DAVID E. DIETRICH

14 JANUARY 1985–29 DECEMBER 2006

"Our Heisman"

David, I began a search for some of your family, friends, or fire department colleagues from Marysville, but no such luck. I reached out to the paper that wrote articles on you and called and messaged the fire department. I wanted someone other than us to talk about you. However, you are our family, and we love you more than any of the others. You have fifty-seven brothers who love you.

It is now 2023, and you would be nearing your first retirement age for the Army. I am positive you would have made a career out of this. You are and were a soldier! When I started therapy for PTSD, one of the counselors suggested I tell your story over and over, out loud, so that I would become desensitized from the trauma of losing you.

"This will help you forget," she said. And with that, I left and immediately asked for a new counselor. I don't want to and will never forget you, my brother. Grief eases over time, and you learn to accept fate and focus on what's in front of you, but every night before I close my eyes, I see you and the others—waiting for me to join you.

You were special and loved, and I miss you; we miss you. Sixteen years later, I still cry every single time I tell your story, and I don't think that will ever change. Keep smiling, and keep doing that Heisman pose. You will forever be our Heisman.

Until Fiddler's Green, brother!

SSG JARED W. ROGERS AND PFC JOSE M. DIAZ JR.

DIED 13 OCTOBER 2021 AND 15 APRIL 2018

S uicide is a hard word to say, mention, or discuss, but it is necessary. Jared and Jose were heroes but chose to end their lives rather than continue to suffer the pain they were dealt. We cannot help ourselves or others until we can say the word "suicide" without shame or embarrassment. It needs attention.

Jared was an amazing soldier, father, and man. He and SSG Storey would crack up laughing while imitating Joe Dirt. We asked Jared, a communication specialist, to fight alongside us in the heart of enemy territory, and he never wavered. Jared, you earned your combat spurs with us, and I look forward to seeing you around the campfire again at the Green.

Jose came to us as a private during our heaviest fighting with the enemy. He learned quick and helped push back and defeat a tough enemy force in Ramadi. We learned that Jose could not handle his liquor when he got drunk on one beer during the Marine Corps birthday celebration on deployment.

We love you both, and I regret I was not there to help when it was needed.

We say suicide is not the answer, yet we allow our heroes to suffer without help. We don't have enough providers in Behavioral Health, and continuity of care sucks.

We must do better!

If you are suffering, please reach out to myself, your teammates, your brothers and sisters in arms:

- ☆ Military OneSource (1-800-342-9647)

- ☆ Veteran's/Military Crisis Line (1-800-273-8255). This is a toll-free, confidential resource, with support 24/7, that connects veterans, service members, including members of the National Guard and Reserve, and their family members with qualified, caring responders.

- ☆ Crisis Chat at https://www.VeteransCrisisLine.net

- ☆ My number (1-703-399-1259)

Outside of Fallujah, Iraq, in September 2003 right before we attacked with the Marines (Operation Long Street).

In Bosnia 1996. Best crew in the platoon. Dan Hudnet, myself, and Vincent Guidera. Vinny was at my retirement ceremony twenty-three years after this deployment.

My command photo as I assumed responsibility as the command sergeant major for 3rd Squadron, 1st Cavalry Regiment, Fort Benning, Georgia.

Route Gremlin destruction, August 2006. Amazingly, everyone survived. SPC Chris Strickland lost a hand and an eye; SPC Matt Wert broke his back.

Our troop guidon. We lived in tents for fourteen months. The guidon stood outside our troop HQ on Camp Ramadi, Iraq

Drill Sergeant Pinion, December 1999–January 2002. One of the
best assignments I ever had.

F Troop, 1st Cav Regiment, Brigade Reconnaissance Troop, 1st Brigade, 1st Armored Division, Camp Ramadi, Iraq.
Fifty-seven soldiers were assigned, and we would lose almost half to injury and death.

"Carrying the Colors": returning from a brigade run. Colors were heavy from all the streamers attached. We were the most decorated cavalry regiment in the Army!
3rd Squadron, 1st Cavalry Regiment, Fort Benning, GA.

Sergeant Pinion, E-5, 1995. Scout Platoon, 4th Battalion, 67th Armor, Friedberg, Germany. Best scout platoon in Europe!

April–May 2006, Northern Iraq after completing a major joint air assault mission with the Iraqi Army. I am on the very right signaling a soldier to take a picture because I thought it would look cool.

Corporal Pinion, Friedberg, Germany, around the 1994–1995 time frame. Taking a break from teaching a sergeant's-time class. Sergeant's time was every Thursday from 0700 to 1200 and gave us uninterrupted time, as a team leader, to train our soldiers on their tasks.

April or May 2006. Immediately after getting inserted during a major joint air assault operation with the Iraqi Army. We were about to do some serious walking all day, searching small villages for enemy. The Iraqi Army did great.

Finished a military tattoo sleeve after retirement. All tattoos are on my right arm and honor my career and our Soldiers.

Baghdad, Iraq, May 2003.

Czech border around 1992–1993. Right after we won another Best Scout Platoon award. Mikey is in this picture, and SFC Gram is on the left.

Route Gremlin

SSG Storey's vehicle after an anti-tank mine strike, two or three weeks before he was killed by another IED.

"Young Guns" crew. SPC Jesus Lugo, driver; SGT Rick Hoffman, gunner; and SFC Dan Pinion, vehicle commander. About to put some "hurt" if necessary.

The best cavalry squadron in the United States Army. 3rd Squadron, 1st Cavalry Regiment, "Blackhawks." I am on the white horse.

Purple Heart and EFMB award ceremony between missions

The day I was appointed to command sergeant major. MG H. R. McMaster appointed me in front of my family and closest friends and colleagues.

ACKNOWLEDGMENTS

This journey was frustrating, scary, amazing, depressing, and incredible all at the same time. It was also long overdue as our soldiers deserved their stories told earlier and more often. I am proud to be a soldier, and despite all my failures and shortcomings, I hope I made a difference to a few around me.

I want to especially acknowledge my wife, Solvig, for her unwavering support on this project. Thank you for leaving me alone to cry when needed and thank you for reaching out to hug me or console me when it appeared life was too hard for me in those moments.

LTG (R) Sean MacFarland for your leadership in the face of the enemy and for your everlasting support and mentorship to myself and my family. Lynda, you are truly an angel and you showed us what right looks like, what genuine care and love should be, and strength when we didn't want to be strong anymore. You both were and are exactly what we needed.

To my colleagues, brothers and sisters in arms, and the unwilling who got pulled into one of my stories. Thank you for listening, laughing, and crying with me and at the end – thank you for repeadedly telling me to put these stories on paper. This book is here because of you all.

To the soldiers: I love you, I miss you, and I can't wait to see you all again, my brothers and sisters.

ABOUT THE AUTHOR

FOR THE MILITARY BUFFS OUT THERE

C ommand Sergeant Major Daniel L. Pinion is a native of Andover, New Jersey. He enlisted in the United States Army delayed entry program on February 5, 1990, and reported for active duty on September 29, 1990. He received his one station unit training at Fort Knox, KY. Upon graduation, he was awarded the military occupation specialty of 19D, cavalry scout.

During his twenty-eight years of service, CSM Pinion has served in numerous leadership positions. His assignments include duty as a gunner and team leader, 2nd Squadron, 9th Cavalry Regiment, Fort Ord, CA; squad leader and section sergeant, 4th Battalion, 67th Armor, 1st Brigade, 1st Armored Division; Scout Platoon Leader's Course instructor, 2nd Squadron, 16th Cavalry Regiment, Fort Knox, KY; drill sergeant and senior drill sergeant, 5th Squadron, 15th Cavalry Regiment, Fort Knox, KY; brigade reconnaissance troop platoon sergeant, F Troop, 1st Cavalry Regiment, 1st Brigade, 1st Armored Division; brigade operations sergeant, 1st Brigade, 1st

Armored Division; first sergeant, F Troop, 1st Cavalry Regiment, 1st Brigade, 1st Armored Division; senior military science instructor, University of Connecticut ROTC; division operations sergeant major, 1st Armored Division, Fort Bliss, TX; battalion operations sergeant major, 3rd Battalion, 41st Infantry Regiment, 1st Brigade, 1st Armored Division; CMF 19 chief career management NCO, United States Army Armor School, Fort Benning, GA; command sergeant major, 3rd Squadron, 1st Cavalry Regiment, Fort Benning, GA; United States Army Europe G3/5/7 sergeant major, HQs USAREUR, Wiesbaden, Germany.

CSM Pinion's military and civilian education includes all levels of the noncommissioned officer education system, Air Assault, Scout Platoon Leader's Course, Instructor Training Course, Pathfinder, Joint Firepower Course, Drill Sergeant School, First Sergeants Course, Senior Enlisted Joint Professional Military Education Course, Command Sergeants Major Course, Command Sergeants Major Development Program–Battalion, "How the Army Runs" for Sergeants Major Force Management Course, and the Executive Leadership Development Course. CSM Pinion is a graduate of the United States Army Sergeants Major Academy, non-resident class thirty-six. CSM Pinion holds a bachelor's degree in liberal studies from Purdue University Global and is currently pursuing his master's degree in executive leadership with Trident University.

CSM Pinion's awards and decoration include the Legion of Merit, Bronze Star Medal (second award), Purple Heart, Meritorious Service Medal (fifth award), Army Commendation Medal (fifth award), Army Achievement Medal (ninth award), Good Conduct Medal (eighth award), National Defense Service Medal (second award), Armed Forces Expeditionary Medal, Armed Forces Service Medal, NATO Medal, Iraq Campaign Medal (two campaign stars), Global War on Terrorism Expeditionary Medal, Global War on Terrorism Service Medal, Presidential Unit Citation (Army), Navy Unit Commendation (Navy), Army Superior Unit Award (third award), Combat Action

Badge, Pathfinder Badge, Air Assault Badge, Drill Sergeant Identification Badge, Wheel Drivers Badge, German Schutzenschnur (Gold), and Draper Armor Leadership Award (third award). CSM Pinion is a member of the Excellence in Armor program since 1992, the Order of the Spur (Silver and Gold), the Order of Saint Maurice (Legionnaire), and the Order of Saint George (Silver Medallion).